Herbert Allen Giles

Synoptical Studies in Chinese Character

Herbert Allen Giles

Synoptical Studies in Chinese Character

ISBN/EAN: 9783337004507

Printed in Europe, USA, Canada, Australia, Japan

Cover: Foto ©Andreas Hilbeck / pixelio.de

More available books at **www.hansebooks.com**

PREFACE.

A STUDY of the written language of China is invariably marred—in its early stages, by an irresistible tendency to confound such characters as resemble each other in general outline and appearance;—later on, even after analysis has been some time called into play, by an inability to retain in the memory without constant application those characters and groups of characters which, differing perhaps only by a dot or a dash, offer little or no handle for association of ideas, but require in each particular instance a separate mnemonic effort. This last difficulty has been felt to some extent by native scholars and obviated in a great measure by the numerous and exhaustive works on orthography which from time to time have been published throughout the empire. Anyone, however, who will turn to the section headed 分毫字辨 in the 問奇一覽, to the third volume of the 字林通考, to K'ang Hsi's chapter on 拼似, or to the 字學舉隅 in either of its four editions, will see at a glance that the stumbling-blocks of the native and the foreigner are very rarely identical; to speak more correctly, that the difficulties experienced by a foreign tyro would be ridiculously out of place in works prepared for the use of graduates desirous only of giving the finishing touches to an almost faultless orthography before becoming candidates for admission into the Han Lin Yüan. For, judging from the collections above mentioned, the blunders of the native are chiefly confined to characters written with the same radical and slightly differing phonetics, the majority of which are, if not actually obsolete, at least very uncommon. The foreign student, on the other hand, is often at a loss to distinguish between any characters at all similar in form which afford no guide through the phonetic or the radical either to their sound or sense. Of such a class are 左 and 右, which would find no place in native collections of like characters. Nor do his troubles end here: he is frequently harassed by characters which bear but a faint resemblance to each other in mere form, but which are alike in sound and tone and perhaps somewhat similar in meaning; he is puzzled by whole families of characters the sound or approximate sound of which he can tell from their possessing a common phonetic, but to the meaning of which the radical in many cases gives not the slightest clue. Several of these phonetic lists have been inserted in this volume at the risk of entrenching upon ground already occupied by M. Callery.

What little there was in native works of practical value to foreign students has been embodied in the present collection, and for the rest, it can hardly be expected that every comparison drawn will meet with general approval. At the same time, it must be borne in mind that all the characters in any group are not necessarily to be compared one with another, though an element of sameness will be found always to pervade each group and frequently a whole series of such which have been placed intentionally in juxtaposition. Further, although this volume begins from the beginning and leaves the student on the threshold of written Chinese, yet a thorough analytical knowledge of all the characters here given will make future classification a comparatively easy matter—and the bitterness of Chinese is past.

The advantages of an Index will, it is hoped, be too patent to need any comment, except perhaps that with its assistance a character may be found even if its sound is unknown, provided that some other character be familiar in the group to which it belongs.

H. A. GILES.

HANKOW CONSULATE,
    28th February, 1874.

SYNOPTICAL STUDIES

IN

CHINESE CHARACTER

1. 人 — *jen²*, a man.
2. 入 — *ju³,⁴*, to enter.
3. 八 — *pa¹*, eight.

---

4. 太 — *t'ai⁴*, excessive. Same as 泰
5. 犬 — *ch'üan³*, a dog.

---

6. 矢 — *shih²*, an arrow.
7. 夫 — *fu¹*, a man.
8. 失 — *shih¹*, to lose.
9. 先 — *hsien¹*, before.

---

10. 天 — *t'ien¹*, heaven.
11. 夭 — *yao¹*, delicate. *winning, tender* Hence 妖 *yao¹*, supernatural.

SYNOPTICAL STUDIES

12 午 — *wu³*, noon. *the 7th of the 12 Branches*

13 牛 — *niu²*, an ox.

14 年 — *nien²*, a year.

---

15 了 — *liao³*, finished.

16 丫 — *ya¹*, forked; a slave-girl.

17 子 — *tzŭ³*, a son. *Conf. 孑 Chieh² = an orphan, alone.* [1st of 12 Branches]

18 予 — *yü²*, I *or* me; to give. But 矛 *mao²*, a spear.

---

19 千 — *ch'ien¹*, a thousand. *Hence 扦 Chien¹ = to graft, &c.*

20 干 — *kan¹*, a shield. *Hence 扞 Han⁴ = to guard, defend. a stem, (天干 = The Ten Stems)*

21 于 — *yü²*, in; at; with &c. *Also written 亐, Cf. 亏* ch/k/q

---

22 手 — *shou³*, the hand.

23 毛 — *mao²*, hair.

---

24 乎 — *hu¹·²*, an interrogative particle.

25 平 — *p'ing²*, level.

26 半 — *pan⁴*, half.

79	心 — $hsin^1$, heart.	
80	必 — $pi^{2,4}$, must.	

81	皿 — min^3, dishes.	
82	血 — $hsieh^3$, blood.	

31	尺 — $ch'ih^3$, a foot.	
32	尼 — ni^2, a nun. Hence 泥 ni^2, mud.	

33	明 — $ming^2$, bright.	
34	朋 — $p'êng^2$, friends.	

35	土 — $t'u^3$, the earth.	
36	士 — $shih^4$, a scholar.	

37	木 — mu^4, wood. Cf. 不 Jun^3 or Yeh^4 quartz powder, Stump of tree	
38	本 — $pên^3$, origin; beginning.	

本 $T'ao^1$ = to enter gladly, in & out.

39 未— *wei*⁴, not. Hence 味 *wei*⁴, flavour; 妹 *mei*⁴, a younger sister.

40 末— *mo*⁴, the end. Hence 沫 *mo*⁴, froth. See No. 681.

---

41 川— *ch'uan*¹·², streams; name of a province.
42 州— *chou*³, a district.

---

43 永— *yung*³, eternal. *cf.* 汞 Hung³ = quicksilver.
44 求— *ch'iu*², to entreat. Hence 救 *chiu*⁴, to save.

---

45 日— *jih*⁴, the sun.
46 曰— *yüeh*¹·⁴, to speak.

---

47 濕 or 溼— *shih*¹, damp.
48 溫— *wên*¹, warm. 温

---

49 夬— *kuai*³, dividing streams. Hence 決 *chüeh*², positively.
50 央— *yang*¹, to request. Hence 英 *ying*¹, English.

IN CHINESE CHARACTER. 5

51 快 — *k'uai⁴*, quick; sharp.
52 怪 — *kuai⁴*, strange.

---

53 缺 — *ch'üeh¹*, a vacancy.
54 卸 — *hsieh⁴*, to discharge cargo.

---

55 夢 — *mêng⁴*, a dream.
56 葬 — *tsang⁴*, to bury.

---

57 奔 — *pên¹*, haste. See no 190: 奔 *jao¹*, to enter gladly.
58 莽 — *mang³*, brambles, tangled, confused; incoherent. also written 莽

---

59 差 — *ch'ai¹*, to send; *ch'a¹*, difference.
60 羞 — *hsiu¹*, shame.

---

61 妾 — *ch'ieh⁴*, a concubine.
62 妄 — *wang⁴*, absurd; extravagant.

---

63 進 — *chin⁴*, to enter.
64 近 — *chin⁴*, near.

65 兄 — *hsiung*¹, an elder brother.
66 兑 — *tui*⁴, to weigh. See No. 1052.

---

67 久 — *chiu*³, a long time. See No. 69.
68 尤 — *yu*², more.
69 允 — *yün*³, to accede to. Also written 尤
70 充 — *ch'ung*¹, to fulfil the duties of. or 克
71 克 — *k'o*⁴, to be able to sustain.

---

72 剋 — *k'o*¹,²,³, to destroy. Also written 尅
73 冠 — *kuan*¹, a cap.
74 寇 — *k'ou*⁴, to plunder.

---

75 田 — *t'ien*², fields.
76 由 — *yu*², from.

---

77 抽 — *ch'ou*¹, to pull out; to levy.
78 押 — *ya*¹,³, to press down; to arrest.

79 細 — hsi¹, fine—not coarse.
80 紬 — ch'ou², silk. So:—
81 袖 — hsiu⁴, a sleeve.
82 柚 — yu⁴, a pumelo.
83 油 — yu², oil.

84 曲 — ch'ü¹,³, crooked; songs.
85 典 — tien³, a dictionary; to mortgage.

86 與 — yü²,³, with; to give.
87 興 — hsing¹,⁴, to begin; to flourish. *Cf.* 嶼 Fei⁴ an ape
88 輿 — yü², a carriage.
89 舉 — chü³, to raise; a graduate.

90 昌 — ch'ang¹, bright; beautiful. Hence 唱 ch'ang⁴, to sing.
91 冒 — mao⁴, to rush blindly; to brave. Hence 帽 mao⁴, a hat.
92 胃 — wei⁴, the stomach. Hence 謂 Wei = to esteem.
93 冑 — chou⁴, a helmet.

94 育 — *yü⁴*, to give birth to; to nourish.
95 肓 — *huang¹*, a vital part of the body.
96 盲 — *mang²*, blind. Also read *wang²*.

---

97 匹 — *p'i²·³*, numerative of horses.
98 四 — *ssŭ⁴*, four.

---

99 西 — *hsi¹*, the west. Cf. 兩 or 西 Hsia⁴ = a cover, to overshadow.
100 酉 — *yu³*, 5 to 7 p.m. the 10th of the Twelve Branches.

---

101 洒 or 灑 — *sa³*, to sprinkle.
102 酒 — *chiu³*, wine.

---

103 栗 — *li⁴*, the chestnut. Cf. 垔 Yin¹: to wall up.
104 粟 — *su²*, maize, or paddy.
105 票 — *p'iao⁴*, a note; a ticket.
106 要 — *yao⁴*, to want. Hence 腰 *yao¹*, the waist.
107 耍 — *shua³*, to play.

108	乂	— i^4, to govern.
109	又	— yu^4, again.
110	叉	— $ch'a^1$, forked.
111	叉	— $chao^3$, claws. Same as 爪. Hence 蚤 $tsao^3$, used for 早 $tsao^3$, early.

112	爪	— $chao^3$ or $chua^3$, claws.
113	瓜	— kua^1, melons &c.

114	仄	— $tsê^4$, oblique.
115	灰	— hui^1, ashes; dust.

116	炭	— $t'an^4$, charcoal.
117	岸	— an^4, the shore.

118	狐	— hu^2, the fox.
119	孤	— ku^1, an orphan.

120	猶	— yu^2, doubtful; as; even &c.
121	獨	— $tu^{2.4}$, only; alone.

10   SYNOPTICAL STUDIES

122 囚 — *ch'iu*², a prison.
123 因 — *yin*¹, a cause. Hence 咽 *yen*¹·⁴, to swallow;
                                 烟 *yen*¹, smoke.
124 困 — *k'un*⁴, tired. Hence 綑 *k'un*³, to bind.
      困 — *Chün*², a granary, spiral
125 恩 — *ên*¹, kindness.
126 思 — *ssŭ*¹, to think.
127 息 — *hsi*¹·², to stop; interest on money.
128 悉 — *hsi*², fully. to know.

---

129 掌 — *chang*³, the palm of the hand.
130 撐 — *ch'êng*¹, to punt.
131 穿 — *ch'uan*¹, to put on [clothes.]
132 裳 — *shang*¹, clothes.
133 常 — *ch'ang*², often.
134 棠 — *t'ang*², a kind of apple-tree.
135 堂 — *t'ang*¹·², a hall.
136 賞 — *shang*³, to bestow. Hence 償 *ch'ang*², to make compensation.
137 嘗 — *ch'ang*², to taste; to try.
138 當 — *tang*¹·⁴, ought; to pawn.
139 富 — *fu*⁴, rich.

IN CHINESE CHARACTER. 11

140 黑 — *hei*¹,³, black.
141 墨 — *mo*⁴, ink.
142 黨 — *tang*³, an association.

---

143 尸 — *shih*¹, a corpse.
144 戶 — *hu*⁴, a door.
  后 *Hou = an Empress.*
145 肩 — *chien*¹, the shoulder.
146 眉 — *mei*², the eyebrows.
147 扁 — *pien*³, flat.
148 雇 — *ku*⁴, to hire. Hence 顧 *ku*⁴, to gaze at.

---

149 僱 — *ku*⁴, to hire. Same as No. 148.
150 偏 — *p'ien*¹, inclined towards.
151 徧 — *pien*⁴, to reach to; to pervade.
  So 篇 *p'ien*¹, leaf of a book.
  編 *pien*¹, to plait; to compose.
  騙 *p'ien*⁴, to cheat.
  鯿

SYNOPTICAL STUDIES

152 冉 — *jan³*, a surname. =tender, weak. Cf. 用 *Yung⁴* = to use
153 再 — *tsai⁴*, again. & 甩 *Shuai¹* = to reject

---

154 幽 — *yu¹*, dark; secluded. 甪 *Lu⁴* = a wild animal,
155 函 — *han²*, a letter. also 圅 & 凾 See next

---

156 亟 — *chi²,⁴*, urgency, promptitude. Hence 極 *chi²*, extreme.
157 丞 — *ch'êng²*, a deputy, an assistant, a courteous term of address to a Lieut. Governor. Same as 承 to receive from a superior.

Hui² = to curve *Chiung³* = lasting, superlative
158 回 — *hui²*, to return. 迴 cf. 逈
or *hui²* Used for *Hui² hui²* = Mohammedan
159 田 — *mien⁴*, the face. Abbreviated form of 面.

---

cf. 囧 *Chiung³*
or 冏 a small window
160 岡 — *kang¹*, top of a hill.
161 罔 — *wang³*, a negative.

---

162 綱 — *kang¹*, a bond; a tie.
163 網 — *wang³*, a net.

IN CHINESE CHARACTER. 13

104 雷 — *lei²*, thunder.
105 電 — *tien⁴*, lightning.

---

106 毘 — *p'i¹*, adjoining.
107 畏 — *wei⁴*, to fear.
108 界 — *chieh¹·⁴*, a boundary; a region. *Chieh* 价 介 夼 Kao to pa the

---

109 異 — *i⁴*, strange; different. See No. 346.
170 暴 — *pao⁴*, cruel; boisterous. Cf. 慕 *mu⁴* = to desire

---

171 冀 — *chi⁴*, to hope. Cf. 糞 *fên-dung*, dirt
172 翼 — *i⁴*, wings; to assist.

---

173 畢 — *pi⁴*, finished.
174 華 — *hua¹·²*, flowery. The lustre of moral cultivation.

---

175 男 — *nan²*, male.
176 勇 — *yung³*, a brave. From 甬 *yung³*, springing forth.
177 舅 — *chiu⁴*, uncle on the mother's side.

14 SYNOPTICAL STUDIES

178 擄 — *lo³*, to plunder; to seize.
179 攄 — *lü³*, to arrange.

---

180 奮 — *fên⁴*, impetuous motion. *See also* 扮 奪 *To²* = to u
181 舊 — *chiu⁴*, old.

---

182 杏 — *hsing⁴*, apricots.
183 杳 — *yao³*, dark; deep. Cf. 沓 *Ta⁴* = babbling, prattling, to pile on; remiss, greedy.
184 查 — *ch'a²*, to investigate.
185 香 — *hsiang¹*, scented.

---

186 呆 — *ai²* or *yai²*, foolish. wicked
187 杲 — *kao³*, the rising sun.
188 枲 — *nieh⁴*, a judge.
189 臭 — *ch'ou⁴*, stinking. Cf. 昊 Ch'ü = a green, the opening of wings
190 皋 — *kao¹*, bank of a river. high, to harangue.
akin with 梟 丁 阜

N.B. 夲 *T'ao'* = ten men (?); to enter gladly; in & out.

| 191 | 烏 | — *wu¹*, a crow; black; how?
| 192 | 鳥 | — *niao³*, birds.
| 193 | 梟 | — *hsiao¹*, to expose criminals' heads.
| 194 | 島 | — *tao³*, islands.
| 195 | 焉 | — *yen¹*, a particle, sometimes interrogative.

| 196 | 刃 | — *jên⁴*, the edge of a knife. 忍 *jen³*, to endure; 認 *jen⁴*, to recognize.
| 197 | 刀 | — *tao¹*, a knife.
| 198 | 刁 | — *tiao¹*, unruly.
| 199 | 力 | — *li⁴*, strength.

| 200 | 深 | — *shên¹*, deep.
| 201 | 染 | — *jan³*, to dye. Cf. 柒 *ch'i¹*, used for 七 seven.
| 202 | 梁 | — *liang¹*, a beam. Cf. No. 196.
| 203 | 粱 | — *liang¹˒²*, millet.

| 204 | 探 | — *t'an¹˒⁴*, to enquire.
| 205 | 控 | — *k'ung⁴*, to accuse.

16 SYNOPTICAL STUDIES

206 茶 — ch'a², tea.
207 荼 — t'u², the old name for tea.
208 菜 — ts'ai⁴, food.

---

209 送 — sung⁴, to send.
210 逆 — ni⁴, undutiful. from 屰 ni⁴ rebellious. (old form) Hence 欮 Chüeh¹ ; 朔 Sho⁴, new m to begin month
211 迭 — tieh², alternate.
212 途 — t'u², a road. See No. 553.

---

213 孕 — yün⁴, pregnant.
214 朶 — to³, the lobe of the ear. Cf. 柔 Jou² Flexible, pliant; elastic, mild, kind

---

215 李 — li³, plums; baggage; a name.
216 季 — chi⁴, the seasons. Tender, young, inferior.
217 委 — wei³, to depute. Truly. Wei-chü = injustice. 委曲
218 秀 — hsiu⁴, elegant; a B. A. degree.
219 禿 — t'u¹, a bald man.

IN CHINESE CHARACTER.   17

220 麥 — *mai*¹, corn. also written 麦
221 桼 — ~~*ch'i*¹: lacquer.~~ original form of next. See No. 226
222 漆 — *ch'i*¹, lacquer, See No. 498. 膝 Hsi¹ = the knee.
223 添 — *t'ien*¹, to add to. adhesive, friendly.

224 梨 — *li*², pears.
225 犁 — *li*², a plough.
226 黎 — *li*², black-haired. From 黍 Shu³ = millet (Will..

227 些 — *hsieh*¹, a few.
228 柴 — *ch'ai*², firewood.
229 紫 — *tzŭ*³, purple.

230 寸 — *ts'un*⁴, an inch.
231 才 — *ts'ai*², ability.

232 村 — *ts'un*¹, a village.
233 材 — *ts'ai*², materials.

234 束 — tz'ŭ⁴, a thorn.
235 束 — shu²·⁴, to bind; to restrain. Hence 速 su², quick.

---

236 刺 — tz'ŭ⁴, to prick, stab; dip; to be hurt; any with cutting, as
237 刺 — la², to cut in two, mangle, hack; inhuman, perverse, retrad
238 勅 or 敕 — ch'ih¹·⁴, Imperial commands.
敕 ... shu⁴, to breathe
239 棘 — chi³, thorns; to prick. 竸 Ching wary & 競 Ching 言 to wrangle
240 棗 — tsao³, dates.

---

241 守 — shou³, to guard.
242 宅 — or toê² chai², private residence. situation, to occupy: House of the dead:
243 它 — t'o¹, he; him. Hence 陀 T'o²
244 宇 — yü³, the universe. a name.

---

245 託 — t'o¹, to request.
246 詫 — ch'a⁴, extravagant talk.
詫

IN CHINESE CHARACTER.   19

247 侍 — *shih⁴*, to wait upon.   From 寺 *ssŭ⁴*, a temple.
248 待 — *tai⁴*, to wait; to behave to.
249 得 — *tê²*, can.   Read *tei*, must.

---

250 恃 — *shih⁴*, to rely upon.
251 持 — *ch'ih²*, to grasp.
252 特 — *t'ê⁴*, especially.

---

253 時 — *shih²*, time.   曉 矓 } *K'ou¹* = sunken eye
254 曉 — *hsiao³*, to know.   撓 *nao²* to scratch

堯 *yao²* Eminent, lofty
嶢 *yao²* Towering, high
僥 *yao²* False, a pigmy

255 弋 — *yi⁴*, to shoot with a bow.
256 戈 — *ko¹*, a spear.

The 5th of the Ten Stems.
257 戊 — *fu⁴*, a character in the 天干. Also read *mou⁴*. luxuriant
258 戍 — *shu⁴*, banishment.   Hence 茂 *mou* or *mao* beauty.
259 戌 — *hsü¹*, 9 to 11 p.m. The 11th of the Twelve Branches
260 戎 — *jung²*, a surname; barbarians.
戒 *Chieh⁴* = to warn, beware

261 賊 — *tsei²*, robbers.
262 賦 — *fu⁴*, to levy taxes.

---

263 紙 — *chih³*, paper.
264 絨 — *jung²*, velveteen.

Cf. 祗 *Chih²* = only, but; to
祗 *Chih²* = rest, great;
Hence

265 氏 — *shih⁴*, a family.   *Cf.* 氐 *Ti³* bottom; 底 *Ti*
266 民 — *min²*, the people.   of
267 良 — *liang²*, virtuous.   底 *Ti* a whe[el]

---

268 眠 — *mien²*, to sleep.
269 眼 — *yen³*, the eyes. From 艮 *kên⁴*, one of the eight diagrams.

---

270 娘 — *niang²*, a woman.
271 浪 — *lang⁴*, waves.
272 狼 — *lang²*, a wolf.

273 狠 or 很 — *hên³*, very.

274 恨 — *hên⁴*, to hate.

275 限 — *hsien⁴*, a limit.

276 根 — *kên¹*, root.

277 銀 — *yin²*, silver.

278 跟 — *kên¹*, the heel; to follow. 吓 跟 Liang² = 佢

---

279 退 — *t'ui⁴*, to push away; to retreat. 腿 *t'ui³*, the leg;
褪 *t'un⁴*, take off.

280 追 — *chui¹*, to pursue.

---

281 昆 — *k'un¹*, an elder brother.

282 皆 — *chieh¹*, all. See No. 929.

283 昏 — *hun¹*, stupid.

284 昏 — *hun¹*, twilight.

The 4th of the Twelve Branches.

285 卯 — *mao³*, 5 to 7 a.m. 仰 *yang³*, to look upwards.
抑 *yi⁴*, to oppress; or.

286 卵 — *luan³*, eggs.

287 印 — *yin*⁴, a seal. Cf. 印 Chiung² = infirm, trouble
288 卽 — *chi*², forthwith &c. 印 Ang² = high, to look up
289 郞 — *lang*², your son. Hence 廊 *lang*², a verandah.
290 朗 — *lang*³·⁴, clear; distinct.
291 旣 — *chi*⁴, finished. Hence 曁 *chi*⁴, together with; 概 *kai*⁴, generally.

---

292 節 — *chieh*²·³, a joint; a festival.
293 筋 — *chin*¹, muscle. From 肋 Lê⁴ or Chin⁴ = the ribs
294 箸 — *chu*⁴, chop-sticks. From 助 Chu⁴ = to assist.

---

295 聊 — *liao*², to depend upon.
296 聯 — *lien*², connected; scrolls.

---

297 昂 — *ang*¹·², to raise &c. See 287
298 昴 — *mao*³, name of a constellation.

---

299 早 — *tsao*³, early.
300 旱 — *han*⁴, drought.
301 皂 — *tsao*⁴, yamên runners; black.

302 泉 — *ch'üan²*, a spring.
303 帛 — *po⁴*, silk. Hence 錦 *chin³*, embroidery.

---

304 綿 — *mien²*, continuous; close texture. Write 棉 cotton.
305 線 — *hsien⁴*, thread; a spy.

---

306 辰 — *ch'ên²*, time. *The 5th of the Twelve Branches.*
307 長 — *chang³*, to grow; *ch'ang²*, long.

---

308 辱 — *ju²·⁴*, to disgrace.
309 脣 or 唇 — *ch'un²*, the lips.

---

310 戚 — *ch'i¹·⁴*, relatives.
311 滅 — *mieh⁴*, to extinguish.

---

312 免 — *mien³*, to avoid. Hence 挽 *wan³*, to draw or pull back; 晚 *wan³*, late.
313 兔 — *t'u¹*, a hare. Hence 冤 *yüan¹*, grievances; 逸 *yi⁴*, to run away. *at large.*
314 勉 — *mien³*, to endeavour.

315 或 — huo⁴, either; or. Hence 國 kuo², a nation;
316 咸 — han², or hsien², all. 域 yü⁴, a boundary;
 蜮 yü⁴, malicious.
317 惑 — huo⁴, suspicion.
318 感 — kan³, gratitude.

---

319 喊 — han³, to call out.
320 緘 — hsien², to seal up.
321 鍼 — chên¹, a needle. Also written 針.

---

322 減 — chien³, to diminish; abbreviated.
323 漸 — chien¹·⁴, gradual.

---

324 凱 — k'ai³, excellent; victorious.
325 剴 — k'ai³, assiduous.
326 獃 — tai¹, an idiot.

---

327 寓 — yü⁴, a dwelling-place. 禹 yü³: loose, free. "One who receives a Kingdom and perfects its work." (Epitaph.)
328 萬 — wan⁴, ten thousand.

329 庚 — kêng¹, a horary character. *The 7th of the Ten Stems.*
330 唐 — t'ang², boasting; name of a dynasty. Hence 糖 t'ang², sugar.
331 康 — k'ang¹, felicity; ease.

332 牀 — ch'uang², a bed.
333 壯 — chuang⁴, strong. Hence 莊 chuang¹, a village; 裝 chuang¹, to pack.
334 狀 — chuang⁴, an accusation. *outward appearance.*
335 戕 — ch'iang¹, to kill.

336 牧 — mu⁴, a pastor. *Cf. 收 Shou¹ = to receive*
337 牡 — mu³, the male of animals.
338 牝 — p'in⁴, the female.

339 庄 — chuang¹, a village. A common form of 莊.
340 床 — ch'uang², a bed. Also written 牀.

341 哉 — tsai¹, an exclamation. *From 戈 Tsai² = s wound*
342 裁 — ts'ai², to cut out [clothes &c.] *截 Chieh² to cut off*
343 栽 — tsai¹, to plant.

344 戟 — *chi³*, a spear.
345 載 — *tsai*³,⁴, to contain; a year.
346 戴 — *tai*⁴, to put on; to wear [a hat.]

---

347 廷 — *t'ing*¹,², the court.
348 延 — *yen*², slow. Hence 涎 *hsien*², saliva; 誕 *tan*⁴, a birth-day.
349 建 — *chien*⁴, to found. See No. 432.

---

350 益 — *i*²,⁴, advantage.
351 盈 — *ying*¹,², abundance.

---

352 姿 — *tzŭ*¹, temper; disposition. 咨
353 恣 — *tzŭ*¹, lewdness.

---

354 庶 — *shu*⁴, the people; nearly. Hence 遮 *chê*¹, to screen.
355 度 — *tu*⁴, a rule; a measure. Hence 渡 *tu*⁴, to ford.

---

356 曆 — *li*⁴, the heavenly bodies. or 歷
357 歷 — *li*⁴, to pass over; lapse of time.

358 晉 — *chin*⁴, to go; name of a dynasty.
359 普 — *p'u*³, universal.
360 菩 — *p'u*², *P'u*-sa.

---

361 剖 — *p'ou*³, to cut open; to decide.
362 部 — *pu*⁴, the [Six] Boards.
363 陪 — *p'ei*², to accompany; to keep a person company.
So 倍 *pei*⁴, fold in four*fold*, ten*fold* &c.;
培 *p'ei*², to add mould to;
賠 *p'ei*², to make compensation.

---

364 沿 — *yen*²,³,⁴, the banks of a river.
365 沼 — *chao*³, a pool.
366 沒 — *mei*² or *mo*⁴ or *mu*²,⁴, not; to perish.
367 浴 — *yü*⁴, to bathe.

---

368 熊 — *hsiung*², a bear. From 能 *nêng*², can.
369 態 — *t'ai*⁴, manner; behaviour.

28　　　　　　SYNOPTICAL STUDIES

370　廛 — ch'an², a market.　Hence 纏 ch'an², to wrap.
371　塵 — ch'ên², dust.
372　麈 — chu³, a kind of deer.

373　炙 — chih¹·⁴, to dry with fire.
374　灸 — chiu⁴, to cauterize.

375　災 — tsai¹, calamity.
376　焚 — fên¹·², to burn.

377　禁 — chin⁴, to prohibit.
378　楚 — ch'u³, clear; distinct.
379　婪 — lan²·³, greedy; avaricious.
380　梵 — fan⁴, Sanskrit.

381　厭 — yen¹·⁴, to dislike.
382　壓 — ya¹·⁴, to suppress; to subject.

383	舜	— *shun*⁴, name of an ancient monarch.
384	舞	— *wu*³·⁴, to posture.

385	麽	— *mo*¹·², an interrogative particle.
386	糜	— *mi*², to destroy.
387	摩	— *mo*¹, to rub; to guess.
388	麾	— *hui*¹, a standard.
389	磨	— *mo*², to grind.

390	丈	— *chang*⁴, a ten-foot measure; a husband.
391	史	— *shih*³, an historian.
392	吏	— *li*⁴, an official; Board of Civil Office.
393	更	— *kêng*¹·⁴, to change; the night-watch.

394	叟	— *sou*³, an old man. Hence 瘦 *shou*⁴, thin.
395	臾	— *yü*², a moment of time.
396	曳	— *i*⁴, to move slowly. Hence 拽 *chuai*¹·⁴, to break; to burst.

397 使 — *shih³*, to use; to employ.
398 便 — *pien⁴*, convenient; *p'ien²*, cheap.

---

399 傳 — *ch'uan²*, to hand down; *chuan⁴*, a history.
       From 專 *chuan¹*, specially. Cf. 惠 *Hui*
400 傅 — *fu⁴*, a tutor. [From 甫 *fu³*, literary name.]
       From 尃 *Fu¹* = to display, extend, *suf¹*
       N.B. orig. form is 尃
401 博 — *po²*, extensive.
402 搏 — *po²*, to strike.
403 縛 — *fu²*, to bind.
404 膊 — *po²·⁴*, the arm.
405 賻 — *fu⁴*, to assist with money.

---

406 薄 — *po²*, thin.
407 簿 — *pu⁴*, an account-book.

---

408 捕 — *pu³*, to seize. ✱ See No. 400
409 補 — *pu³*, to make up a deficiency.
410 鋪 — *p'u⁴*, to spread out.
411 舖 — *p'u⁴*, a shop.

IN CHINESE CHARACTER. 31

412 偷 — *t'eu¹*, to steal.
413 倫 — *lun²*, the [five] relationships.

---

414 諭 — *yü¹*, an Edict. From *yü²* 俞 to respond, assent.
415 論 — *lun²,⁴*, to discuss.

---

416 輸 — *shu¹*, to lose [games &c.]
417 輪 — *lun²*, a wheel.
418 轉 — *chuan³,⁴*, to turn round. See No. 399.

---

419 軍 — *chün¹*, military.
420 葷 — *hun¹*, animal food.
420a 暈 — *yün¹,⁴*, vapour; giddiness.
421 渾 — *hun²,³*, the whole of.
422 揮 — *hui¹*, to shake. to brandish.
423 運 — *yün⁴*, to convey.
424 蓮 — *lien²*, the water-lily. From 連 *lien¹,²*, connected.

425 到 — tao⁴, to arrive. Cf. 郅 Chih⁴ = to ascend, flourishing, very
426 利 — li⁴, sharp; interest on money.
427 列 — lieh⁴, to put in order. Hence 烈 lieh⁴, virtuous.

---

428 倒 — tao³, to fall down; tao⁴, to pour out.
429 俐 — li⁴, clever.
430 例 — li⁴, bye-laws.
431 律 — lü⁴, statutes.
432 健 — chien⁴, strong.

---

433 玄 — hsüan², black. Now read yüan².
434 糸 — mi⁴, silk.
435 系 — hsi¹·⁴, connected.
436 矣 — i³, a particle.
437 妥 — t'o³, safe.
438 采 — ts'ai³, to pick. Cf. 釆 Pien⁴, to part + distinguish
439 奚 — hsi¹, how? why?
440 受 — shou⁴, to receive.
441 愛 — ai⁴, to love.

442 係— hsi¹,⁴, to be.
443 俟— ssŭ⁴, to wait.
444 後— hou¹, after; behind.
445 侯— hou², a nobleman.   猴 hou² = a monkey
446 候— hou⁴, to wait.
447 條— t'iao², a numerative; a clause.   滌 ti², clean.
448 脩— hsiu⁴, teacher's salary.
449 修— hsiu⁴, to repair; to adorn. or 俻 cf 俻 Pei⁴ = to prep
450 俻 or 備— pei⁴, to prepare. or 葡: cf 葡 P'u² = The vine
                                    fr. 匍 P'u² = to craw
451 索— so¹, to extort.   cf. 匐 P'u⁴ = Fall
452 素— su⁴, vegetable diet. commonly: empty: plain.
453 表— piao³, evident; a watch. cf. 麦 mai⁴ = corn.

454 肴— yao², food.
455 希— hsi¹, to hope; few.   or 布

456 帥— shuai⁴, a commander.
457 師— shih¹, a teacher.

458 飾 — *shih¹*, ornament.
459 飭 — *ch'ih¹·⁴*, to order.

---

460 亨 — *hêng¹·²* = to provide; successful, passing through. The old form of 烹 *p'eng¹*, to boil.
461 享 — *hsiang³*, to enjoy.
462 亭 — *t'ing²*, a shed; perpendicular.
463 亮 — *liang⁴*, bright; dawn. See No. 560.

---

464 敦 — *tun¹*, sterling; substantial. Cf. 教 *Chiao¹·⁴* to teach
465 郭 — *kuo¹*, suburbs.

---

466 執 — *chih²*, to grasp. Cf. 藝 *i⁴* = skill, art
467 孰 — *shu²*, who? Cf. *chiu⁴* 就 then.

---

468 熱 — *jê⁴*, hot.
469 熟 — *shu²* or *shou²*, ripe; cooked; intimate.

---

470 塾 — *shu²*, a school-room.
471 墩 — *tun¹*, a mound or hillock.

IN CHINESE CHARACTER. 35

472 埝 — *tien*⁴, to pay; a cushion.
473 勢 — *shih*⁴, influence.
474 褻 — *hsieh*⁴, rags; to treat with disrespect.
475 藝 — *i*⁴, skill; the [six] elegant accomplishments.

---

476 亦 — *i*¹·²·³, also.
477 赤 — *ch'ih*¹·⁴, naked; red.
478 郝 — *hao*⁴, a surname.
479 赦 — *shê*⁴, pardon.

---

480 脊 — *chi*³, the back-bone; a ridge.
481 眷 — *chüan*⁴, family.
482 春 — *ch'un*², spring.
483 舂 — *ch'ung*¹, to pound.

---

484 奉 — *fêng*⁴, to receive from a superior.
485 奏 — *tsou*⁴, to address the Emperor. Hence 湊 *ts'ou*⁴, to collect together.
486 秦 — *ch'in*², name of a dynasty. Hence 臻 *chên*¹, to arrive.
487 泰 — *t'ai*⁴, same as 太. See No. 4.

488 巷 — *hsiang*⁴, a street.   So 港 *chiang*³, streams.
489 卷 — *chüan*³,⁴, archives.   So 倦 *chüan*⁴, tired;
                                    捲 *chüan*³, to roll up;
                                    圈 *ch'üan*¹,⁴, a circle.
490 券 — *ch'üan*⁴, a deed or bond.
491 拳 — *ch'üan*², the fist. *love, amity.*
    拲 — *kung*³, to fasten a prisoner's hands [in a board].
492 椿 — *ch'un*¹, name of a tree; a father.
493 椿 — *chuang*¹, a post.

{ 椿萱並茂 }

---

494 賸 — *shêng*⁴, surplus.
495 謄 — *t'êng*², to copy.
496 勝 — *shêng*⁴, to be worthy of; to be victorious.
497 騰 — *t'êng*², to ascend.
498 膝 — *hsi*¹, the lap.   See No. 222. *From* 桼 *Ch'i¹ = lacquer*
499 籐 — *t'êng*², rattan.

---

500 癸 — *kuei*³, a horary character. *The 10ᵗʰ of the Ten Stems.*
501 祭 — *chi*⁴, to sacrifice. Hence 察 *ch'a*¹,², to investi-
                                    gate.
502 詧 — *ch'a*², to investigate.

[Continued—

IN CHINESE CHARACTER.

Continued—

503 登 — têng¹, to ascend. Hence 鐙 teng⁴,
　　　　　　　　　　　　　　and 燈 têng¹, a

504 凳 — teng⁴, a stool.

505 發 — fa¹, to send forth.

---

506 揆 — k'uei², to guess. *to estimate.*

507 撥 — po¹, to push back; to separate. *to d*

---

508 莫 — mo⁴, not. See No. 520 et seq.

509 革 — ko², leather; to degrade.

510 草 — ts'ao³, plants. See No. 299.

---

511 勒 — lo⁴, to restrain; to extort.

512 勤 — ch'in², diligent.

513 鄞 — ying², the district in which Ningpo i

514 覲 — chin³, to see the Emperor.

---

515 親 — ch'in¹,⁴, near; relatives.

516 新 — hsin¹, new. So 薪 hsin¹, teacher's

517 報 — pao⁴, to report.

SYNOPTICAL STUDIES

518 動 — *tung⁴*, to move. See No. 549.
519 勛 or 勳 — *hsün¹*, meritorious public service.

---

520 慕 — *mu⁴*, to desire. See No. 508. Cf. 暴 *pao⁴* cruel.
521 暮 — *mu⁴*, evening.
522 摹 — *mo²*, to imitate [writing, drawing &c.]
523 募 — *mu⁴*, to appeal for subscriptions &c. enlist.
524 幕 — *mu⁴*, a secretary.
525 墓 — *mu⁴*, a grave.

---

526 基 — *chi¹*, a foundation. See No. 1082. Cf. 基 *chi¹* very
527 塞 — *sai⁴*, to stop up; cork. From 寒 *hsia⁴* = to fill
528 寒 — *han²*, cold.
529 賽 — *sai⁴*, to rival. Cf. 謇 *chien³* = to stutter, stra
530 寨 — *chai⁴*, a fort. Cf. 搴 *chien¹* = to pluck, on
531 蹇 — *chien³*, lame. & 蹇 *chien³* = cymbal s

IN CHINESE CHARACTER. 39

532 歎 — *t'an*⁴, to sigh.
533 艱 — *chien*¹, difficult.
534 難 — *nan*²,⁴, difficult.
535 雜 — *tsa*², miscellaneous.

---

536 乖 — *kuai*², strange.
537 乘 — *shêng*⁴, a chariot; to mount. Contracted to 乘 H
538 垂 — *ch'ui*², to hang down. To condescend; to bow.

---

539 剩 or 賸 — *shêng*⁴, surplus.
540 郵 — *yu*², a place where couriers change horses.

---

541 秉 — *ping*³, to grasp. oversee, direct.
542 兼 — *chien*¹, together with. Hence:— *Contracted from

---

543 廉 — *lien*², modest; honest.
544 簾 — *lien*², a bamboo screen.
545 嫌 — *hsien*², odium.
546 謙 — *ch'ien*¹, respectful; humble.
547 鎌 — *lien*², a sickle.
548 歉 — *ch'ien*¹, deficient.

40 SYNOPTICAL STUDIES

549 重 — chung⁴, heavy; ch'ung², again; repeated.
550 熏 — hsün¹, vapour. See No. 519.
551 董 — tung³, 'a manager. *a village elder*: to influence for good, to store up
552 薰 — hsün¹, pleasant smells; to asphyxiate. [古董 = cur

---

553 余 — yü², I; me. Hence 除 ch'u², to subtract;
                                 餘 yü², surplus.
554 佘 — shê², a surname. *Shê Shan Islands.*
555 奈 — nai⁴, resource; alternative.
556 柰 — nai⁴, name of a fruit. Used for the above.

---

557 宋 — sung⁴, name of a dynasty: *a dwelling*
558 宗 — tsung¹, ancestors: *a sort, kind*
559 完 — wan², finished.
560 亮 — liang⁴, bright; dawn. See No. 463. *Cf. 壳 K'o⁴: rest*
561 崇 — ch'ung², noble. *lofty. Cf. 岂 Ch'i³: how?* 壹 *a bar musi*
562 祟 — sui⁴, evil spirits &c. *apparently also written* 素 *& in that form confused with* 柰 *nai⁴, 556* 隸

Apparently also confused with 耆*. Since* 斁 *chui¹ tui¹ a parasite, was formerly written* 斁 *and* 贕. *N.B.* 敖 ᵐ'Ao² = *to ramble, proud.*

563 石 — *shih²*, a stone.
564 右 — *yu⁴*, the right hand.
565 左 — *tso³*, the left hand.
566 友 — *yu³*, a friend.

---

567 布 — *pu⁴*, piece goods.
568 市 — *shih⁴*, a market. Hence 鬧 *nao⁴*, to make a noise.
569 巿 — *fei⁴*. Hence 肺 *fei⁴*, the lungs; 沛 *p'ei⁴*, rainy &c.

---

570 反 — *fan³*, back again; to rebel.
571 皮 — *p'i²*, skin.

572 扳 — *pan¹*, to take out [teeth.] *P'an¹*, to pull down.
573 拔 — *pa²*, to pull out [corks &c.] 跋 *po⁴*, to travel.
574 披 — *p'ei*¹·⁴ or *p'i*¹·³, to open; to throw over the shoulders.

---

575 被 — *pei⁴*, bed-clothes; to suffer.
576 坡 — *p'o¹*, a steep bank.

[Continued—

Continued—

577 波 — po^1, waves.
578 玻 — po^1, glass.
579 破 — $p'o^4$, broken; torn.
580 頗 — $p'o^1$, in some degree.

---

581 授 — $shou^4$, to give to.
582 援 — $yüan^2$, to lead; to rescue.

---

583 疋 — $p'i^3$, a *piece* of cloth &c.
584 定 — $ting^4$, fixed.

---

585 足 — tsu^2, the foot; enough.
586 是 — $shih^4$, is.

---

587 捉 — cho^1, to seize.
588 提 — $t'i^2$, to lift up.
589 捷 — $chieh^2$, promptitude.

590 苦 — k'u³, bitter. See No. 1271.
591 若 — jo⁴, if. See No. 564.

---

592 諾 — no³, to answer.
593 諸 — chu¹, all.

---

594 書 — shu¹, books.
595 晝 — chou⁴, day-time.
596 畫 — hua⁴, to draw or paint.
597 盡 — chin⁴, exhausted; entirely.

---

598 儘 — chin³, all; wholly. Used for the preceding.
599 僅 — chin³, hardly; just. See No. 512.

---

600 奠 — tien⁴, to sacrifice.　鄭 chêng⁴, worthy;
　　　　　　　　　　　　　　擲 chih¹,⁴, to fling away.
601 尊 — tsun¹, honourable; aged.

---

602 遵 — tsun¹, obediently to.
603 導 — tao⁴, to lead.

604 番 — *fan*$^{1.2}$ or *p'an*^{1}, a time *or* turn; foreign.
605 蕃 — *fan*^{2}, luxuriant.
606 審 — *shên*$^{3.4}$, to investigate.
607 潘 — *p'an*^{1}, name of a place.
608 藩 — *fan*$^{1.2}$, Commissioner of Finance; the Li-*fan*-yüan.
609 籓 — *fan*^{2}, a fence.
610 播 — *po*$^{3.4}$, to throw away; to dupe.
611 繙 — *fan*^{1}, to translate.
612 嬸 — *shên*$^{3.4}$, father's younger brother's wife.
613 翻 — *fan*^{1}, to turn over.

---

614 雍 — *yung*^{3}, harmonious. So 擁 *yung*^{3}, crowding round.
615 雄 — *hsiung*^{2}, the male of birds; a hero.

---

616 相 — *hsiang*$^{1.4}$, mutual.
617 想 — *hsiang*^{3}, to think.
618 箱 — *hsiang*^{1}, a box.

IN CHINESE CHARACTER.   45

619 緣 — *yüan²*, a cause.
620 綠 — *lü⁴*, green. So:—

621 祿 — *lu⁴*, happiness.
622 碌 — *lu⁴*, rocky.
623 錄 — *lu⁴*, to transcribe.

篆 Chuan⁴ Seal character.
from 彖 Tuan⁴ = hedgehog. application of diagrams to explain.
from 彔 Lu⁴ = to carve

---

624 業 — *yeh⁴*, property; already. But:—
625 僕 — *p'u²*, a servant.
626 撲 — *p'u²*, to strike.
627 樸 — *p'u²*, sincere.

From 業 Pu⁴ a thicket, case for rods.

丵 Hsio⁴·Pu⁴ or Fu⁴·
業 Pu⁴ [ts'u, sh]
業 Yeh⁴
叢 Tsung²

628 蕭 — *su²·⁴*, awe.
629 蕭 — *hsiao¹*, decay.
630 簫 — *hsiao¹*, a flageolet.
631 繡 — *hsiu⁴*, to embroider.
632 鏽 — *hsiu⁴*, rust.

對 Tui⁴
鑿 Tso⁴·
鑿 Tso⁴ Tsao²
corr. miller
鑿

633 默 — *mo⁴*, silently.
634 黔 — *ch'ien²*, black-haired; Kwei-chow.
635 點 — *tien³*, a point; to light. See No. 1272.

---

636 賀 — *ho⁴*, to congratulate.
637 貿 — *mao⁴*, trade. to barter, also read mou.

---

638 累 — *lei²⁻³⁻⁴*, to bind together; to implicate.
639 畧 — *lüeh³⁻⁴*, a little; items; sections.

---

640 纍 — *lei²*, to twist.
641 壘 — *lei³*, a rampart.
642 疊 — *tieh²*, often.

---

643 紀 — *chi⁴*, period of 12 years; to record. See No. 966.
644 級 — *chi²*, degrees of rank. See No. 1231.

---

645 迫 — *p'o¹*, urgent.
646 逼 — *pi¹*, to force; to bully.

647 功 — *kung*¹, meritorious service.
648 攻 — *kung*¹, to attack.

---

649 罵 — *ma*⁴, to curse.
650 篤 — *tu*³, to give due weight to.

---

651 貌 — *mao*⁴, the countenance.
652 藐 — *miao*³, to despise.

---

653 繼 — *chi*⁴, succession; an heir.
654 斷 — *tuan*⁴, to decide.

---

655 彊 — *chiang*¹, strong.
656 疆 — *chiang*¹, a boundary.

---

657 冥 — *ming*², dark; Hades.
658 宴 — *yen*⁴, a feast.
659 晏 — *yen*⁴, serene; late.

660 躬 — *kung*¹, oneself.
661 射 — *shê*⁴, to shoot with a bow.

---

662 斜 — *hsieh*², oblique.
663 叙 — *hsü*⁴, to chat.

---

664 狄 — *ti*², a surname.
665 秋 — *ch'iu*², autumn.

---

666 霸 — *pa*⁴, violence; force.
667 羈 — *chi*¹, to delay.
668 羈 — *chi*¹, a bridle. Used for the preceding.

---

669 復 — *fu*²,⁴, to reply; again.
670 覆 — *fu*⁴, to reply; to turn upside down.

---

671 欸 — *k'uan*³, a clause., *Items*.
672 疑 — *i*², to suspect.

673 短 — *tuan*³, short.
674 矮 — *ai*³, a dwarf. short (of men): low (of things) opp.

675 代 — *tai*⁴, instead of; a generation.
676 伐 — *fa*¹·², to punish; to prune.
677 伏 — *fu*², to lie prostrate; concealed.
678 付 — *fu*⁴, to send; to pay. to give or deliver to. Hence 符 *fu*², to tally; 府 *fu*³, a Prefecture.
679 休 — *hsiu*¹, to stop; to divorce.

680 沐 — *mu*⁴, to wash; to receive favours.
681 沫 — *mo*⁴, froth. See No. 40.
682 淋 — *lin*⁴, water dripping.

683 貸 — *tai*⁴, to pardon.
684 貨 — *huo*⁴, merchandize.

685 夕 — *hsi*¹·², evening.
686 歹 — *tai*³, bad.

687 名 — *ming²*, a name.
688 各 — *ko²·³*, each; every; self. See No. 705.

---

689 仝 — *t'ung²*, a common form of 同.
690 全 — *ch'üan²*, all.
691 金 — *chin¹*, gold.
692 舍 — *shê⁴*, a cottage.

---

693 合 — *ho²*, to agree with. Hence 給 *kei³*, to give.
694 台 — *t'ai²*, a term of respect.
Hence 始 *shih³*, the beginning;
胎 *t'ai¹*, the womb.

---

695 抬 — *t'ai²*, to carry.
696 拾 — *shih²*, to pick up; to put in order; ten.
697 拴 — *shuan¹*, to tie up.
698 捨 — *shê⁴*, to part with.

---

699 冶 — *yeh³*, to melt; meretricious, enticing
700 治 — *chih⁴*, to govern.
701 洽 — *hsia⁴*, to harmonize.

702 答 — *ta*¹·², to reply. *Cf.* 荅 *Ja*²: to sustain, un[...]
703 筓 — *ch'ih*¹·²·⁴, to beat with the smaller bamboo.

---

704 貽 — *i*², to bequeath; to cause.
705 賂 — *lu*⁴, bribes.

---

706 格 — *ko*², a limit; to scrutinize.
707 恪 — *ch'uo*⁴, respect; attention.
708 怯 — *ch'ieh*⁴, nervousness.
709 怡 — *i*², harmony.
710 恰 — *ch'ia*⁴, luckily.

---

711 含 — *han*² or *hên*², to hold in the mouth; indistinct.
712 念 — *nien*⁴, to think; to read.
713 衾 — *ch'in*², a shroud; bed-clothes.
714 衿 — *chin*¹, the front flap of a Chinese coat.

---

715 准 — *chun*³, to allow; to receive.
716 淮 — *huai*², name of a river. Hence 匯 *hui*³·⁴, bill of exchange.
717 準 — *chun*³, a measure; a standard.

718 套 — *t'ao⁴*, a case *or* covering.
719 奪 — *to²*, to seize. See No. 160. 奮 Fên⁴ = impetuosity

---

720 東 — *tung¹*, east.
721 柬 — *chien³*, a visiting-card. Hence:—

---

722 揀 — *chien³*, to choose.
723 練 — *lien⁴*, to drill; to practice.
724 鍊 — *lien⁴*, to fuse metals.
725 諫 — *chien³,⁴*, to remonstrate.

---

726 陣 — *chên⁴*, ranks; the line of battle.
727 陳 — *ch'ên²*, old.

---

728 之 — *chih¹*, sign of the genitive case.
729 乏 — *fa⁴*, destitute; tired. Hence 泛 *fan⁴*, to float.

---

730 眨 — *chan³*, twinkling [of an eye.]
731 貶 — *pien³*, to censure.

IN CHINESE CHARACTER.   53

732 交 — *chiao¹*, to hand over; intimacy.

733 夾 — *chia¹*, double.

734 來 — *lai²*, to come. *Cf.* 卒 *Tsu²* = a soldier, *suddenly, entire*, [also written 卆]

735 爽 — *shuang³*, bright.

---

736 狡 — *chiao³*, crafty. So 絞 *chiao³*, to strangle.

737 狹 or 陝 — *hsia²*, narrow.
    So 俠 *hsia²*, a hero;
    挾 *chia¹'²*, to take under the arm.
    But 陝 *shan³*, the province of Shensi.

---

738 効 — *hsiao⁴*, to exert oneself.

739 效 — *hsiao⁴*, to imitate; improvement.

740 郊 — *chiao¹*, waste ground outside a city.

---

741 仔 — *tzŭ³*, carefully. *Conf.* 伃 *Yü* = handsome, *also written* 好 *Yü*

742 存 — *ts'un²*, to keep. *Conf.* 序 *Hsü* = in order, series. *Conf.* 好 *Hao*

---

743 在 — *tsai⁴*, to be.

744 任 — *jen²*, official responsibility.

Continued—

Continued—

745 住 — *chu⁴*, to dwell; to stop.
746 往 — *wang*³⁴, to go.

747 信 — *hsin⁴*, a letter; good faith.
748 佳 — *chia¹*, beautiful.
749 隹 — *chui¹*, birds.

---

750 售 — *shou⁴*, to sell.
751 焦 — *chiao¹*, burnt.
752 集 — *chi²*, collected together. Cf. 隼 *Shun³* (a falcon) [also written 鶉]

---

753 雁 or 鴈 — *yen⁴*, a wild goose.
754 應 — *ying*¹⁴, ought.
755 鷹 — *ying⁴*, hawk; eagle. old form 雁

---

756 馮 — *fêng²*, a surname.
757 憑 — *p'ing²*, to rely on.

758 哀 — *ai¹*, to pity.
759 衷 — *chung¹*, equitable.
760 衰 — *shuai¹*, to fade.
761 裒 — *p'ou¹*, to deduct from.
762 袞 — *kun³*, robes. Hence 滚 *kun³*, boiling.
763 袁 — *yüan²*, long garments; a surname.

---

764 裏 or 裡 — *li³*, inside.
765 裹 — *kuo³*, to bind up.

---

766 襄 — *hsiang¹*, to aid.
767 囊 — *nang²*, a bag.

---

768 壞 — *huai⁴*, to spoil.
769 壤 — *jang²·³*, a boundary; a place, conterminous, a

---

770 遠 — *yüan³*, far. See No. 763.
771 還 — *huan²*, still; to repay.

772 辛 — hsin¹, bitter. The 8th of the Ten Stems. cf. 辛
773 幸 — hsing⁴, lucky. Cf. 幸 or 䒔 Ja²: a new born lamb, easy! and 䒔 Hsio⁴ Pu⁴ Tu⁴ : bushy. Hen see no. 624-627
774 牢 — lao², a prison.
775 宰 — tsai³, to govern; to slay.

776 辜 — ku¹, crime; ingratitude.
777 喜 — hsi³, joy. Cf. 善 Shan⁴ virtuous.
778 嘉 — chia¹, excellent.

779 壹 — yi¹, one.
780 臺 — t'ai², a terrace.

781 藉 — chieh⁴, to rely on. cf. 耤 Chieh = to till, or plough.
782 籍 — chi²,³, books; native place.

783 參 — ts'an¹, to join, visit. impeach; ts'ên¹, irregular. Also written 叄
784 叄 — san¹,⁴, three.

785 月 — *yüeh⁴*, the moon..
786 月 — *jou⁴*, flesh.
787 丹 — *tan¹*, red.
788 舟 — *chou¹*, a boat.

789 船 — *ch'uan²*, a ship.
790 般 — *pan¹*, a kind; a class.

791 股 — *ku³*, a band [of robbers]; a share. The buttocks
792 服 — *fu²*, clothes; to submit to.

793 井 — *ching³*, a well.
794 升 — *shêng¹*, a pint; to rise towards.
795 弁 — *pien⁴*, military officials. See no. 70, 允 *yün³*:
796 并 — *ping⁴*, together. & 幷 *chou³*:

797 刑 — *hsing²*, punishment.
798 形 — *hsing²*, form; appearance.

799 刊 — *k'an*¹,³, to engrave.
800 判 — *p'an*⁴, to judge.
801 叛 — *p'an*⁴, to rebel.

---

802 製 — *chih*⁴, to make. From 制 *chih*⁴, laws; to govern.
803 掣 — *ch'ih*⁴ [*ch'ê*⁴], to hinder, to pull towards one.

---

804 叵 — *p'o*³, cannot, do not. Said to be 轉注 form of 可
805 巨 — *chü*⁴, vast; numerous. See No. 813.
806 臣 — *ch'ên*² , a minister. Cf. 臣 ʃ² = the chin

---

807 官 — *kuan*¹, mandarin. Cf. 㠯 or 以 ʃ³ = in order to,
808 宦 — *huan*⁴, an official.
809 菅 — *chien*¹, grass; weeds.
810 管 — *kuan*³, to manage.

---

811 歐 — *ou*¹, to vomit. ⎫ From 區 *ch'ü*¹, a dwelling;
812 毆 — *ou*¹,³, to beat. ⎭ small.

813 拒 — *chü*⁴, to ward off, to resist illegally
814 距 — *chü*⁴, distant from.
815 詎 — *chü*⁴, contrary to expectation.
816 矩 — *chü*¹⁻⁴, square; custom.

---

817 弔 — *tiao*⁴, to mourn.
818 弟 — *ti*⁴, a younger brother.   剃 *t'i*⁴, to shave; 梯 *t'i*¹, a ladder.
819 弗 — *fu*², not. Cf. 弗 Ch'an³ or Chuan³ = a spit or gridiron.
820 夷 — *i*², a barbarian.   Hence 胰 *yi*², soap.
821 笫 — *tzŭ*³, a bed.
822 第 — *ti*⁴, a series.

---

823 姊 — *tzŭ*³, an elder sister.
824 娣 — *ti*⁴, a younger sister.
825 姨 — *i*², wife's sisters.

---

826 佛 — *fo*², Buddha.
827 彿 — *fu*²⁻⁴, resembling.

828 仿 — *fang³*, according to.

829 彷 — *fang³*, resembling.

---

830 壬 — *jen²*, The 9th of the Jen Stems. an astronomical character. See No. 893.

831 王 — *wang²*, a prince. cnf. 王京 = good, complete.

832 玉 — *yü⁴*, jade.

---

833 呈 — *ch'êng²*, to present a petition.

834 皇 — *huang²*, the Emperor.

835 星 — *hsing¹*, stars.

---

836 嬴 — *ying²*, to expand.

837 贏 — *ying²*, to win.

---

838 毀 — *hui³*, to break to pieces.

839 段 — *tuan⁴*, a paragraph; satin.

840 叚 — *chia³*, to borrow. Hence 假 *chia³,⁴*, false; 暇 *hsia²*, leisure; 瑕 *hsia²*, a speck; 遐 *hsia²*, remote.

[Continued—

Continued—

841 殷 — yin^1, sincere.
842 殿 — $tien^4$, a palace; rear-guard.

---

843 遊 or 游 — yu^2, to roam.
844 邀 — yao^1, to invite.
845 激 — chi^1, emotion.
846 繳 — $chiao^3$, to pay. *hand back, return.*
847 檄 — hsi^4, a despatch.

---

848 徹 — $ch'ê^4$, to penetrate.
849 徼 — $chiao^3$, luckily. Also read yao^1. *Interchanged with*
850 傲 — ao^4, proud.
851 徵 — $chêng^1$, to levy, *to attest, hear, witness to.*
852 微 — $wei^{1.2}$, minute; small.
853 徽 — hui^1, province of An-*hui*.
854 懲 or 懲 — $ch'êng^{2.3}$, to punish.

---

855 撤 — $ch'ê^4$, to remove. So 轍 $chê^2$, a cart-rut.
856 撒 — $sa^{1.2.3}$, to scatter.

857 鮮 — hsien¹·³, fresh; few.
858 鮮 or 解 — chieh³·⁴ and hsieh⁴, to cut; a surname. *to release, extricate, dispel*
read Chiai⁴ = to forward, transmit as a prisoner

---

859 孔 — k'ung³, Confucius.
860 乳 — ju³·⁴, milk.

---

861 浮 — fu², to float.
862 淨 — ching⁴, clean.

---

863 員 — yüan², an official.
864 買 — mai³, to buy.
865 賣 — mai⁴, to sell.
866 賈 — ku³, a merchant. Also read chia³. Hence 價 chia⁴, price.
867 貴 — kuei⁴, dear; honourable. See No. 909.
868 貫 — kuan⁴, connected. Hence 慣 kuan⁴, accustomed to.
869 責 — tsê²·⁴, to punish; responsibility.
870 靑 — ch'ing¹, dark blue.

871 清 — *ch'ing¹*, pure.
872 靖 — *ching⁴*, peace; quietness.
873 猜 — *ts'ai¹·³*, to guess.
874 情 — *ch'ing¹·²*, the passions. *or, circumstances*
875 晴 — *ch'ing²*, a clear sky.
876 睛 — *ching¹*, the eye.
877 靜 — *ching⁴*, the stillness of non-motion.
878 請 — *ch'ing³*, to request.
879 精 — *ching¹*, essence; animal spirits &c.

---

880 瀆 — *tu³*, to annoy.
881 犢 — *tu²·³*, a calf.
882 牘 — *tu³*, written documents.
883 續 — *hsü⁴*, continuous.
884 贖 — *shu²*, to atone for; to take out of pawn. Cf.
885 讀 — *tu²*, to study. 覿 *Ti²: to see face to face, audience.*

64 SYNOPTICAL STUDIES

886 澤 — *tsê*², soaked; softened; enriched.
887 擇 — *tsê*², to choose.
888 繹 — *yi*⁴, to lay before; to proceed in order.
889 釋 — *shih*²·⁴, to release.
890 鐸 — *to*², a bell.
891 譯 — *yi*⁴, to translate.
892 驛 — *yi*⁴, a postal stage.

---

893 賃 — *lin*⁴, to rent a house. See No. 830.
894 債 — *chai*⁴, debts.
895 漬 — *tzŭ*⁴, dirt; a dirty mark.
896 績 — *chi*¹·⁴·⁷, to twist. *services, merit*.
897 積 — *chi*¹·², to accumulate.
898 稽 — *chi*¹, to investigate. *keep the best. Chi-liu = [to detain]*.

---

899 寬 — *k'uan*¹, broad.
900 賓 or 賔 — *pin*¹, a guest.
901 實 — *shih*², true. From No. 868.

902 勸 — ch'üan⁴, to admonish.
903 歡 — huan¹, to rejoice.
904 觀 — kuan⁴, to look at.
905 灌 — kuan⁴, to force a person [to drink &c.]
906 權 — ch'üan², authority.

---

907 護 — hu⁴, to guard.
908 獲 — huo⁴, to seize.

---

909 遺 — i², to leave behind; to lose. See No. 867.
910 遣 — ch'ien³, to send.

---

911 捐 — chüan¹, to pay money.
912 損 — sun³, to damage.
913 揖 — yi⁴, a Chinese salutation.

---

914 絹 — chüan⁴, lustring; a pocket-handkerchief.
915 緝 — ch'i¹, to seize. Also read chi¹.

916 尚 — *shang²ꞏ⁴*, still; nearly.
917 南 — *nan²*, south.
918 商 — *shang¹*, a merchant.
919 商 — *shih* or *ti*. Hence:—

920 摘 — *chai¹*, to pull off.
921 滴 — *ti¹*, water dropping.
922 謫 — *tsê⁴*, to banish.
923 適 — *shih⁴*, suddenly; by chance.

924 敞 — *ch'ang³*, open; level.
925 敝 — *pi⁴*, vulgar; humble.
926 敵 — *ti¹ꞏ²*, an enemy.

927 陞 — *shêng¹*, to be promoted.
928 陛 — *pi⁴*, steps to a throne or dais.
929 階 — *chieh¹*, steps to a house &c. See No. 282.

IN CHINESE CHARACTER. 67

930 陸 — *lu*⁴, by land; used for the number *six*.
931 陵 — *ling*², the Imperial tombs. So 凌 *ling*², an icicle; to insult.
932 降 — *chiang*⁴, to degrade. *Hsiang*², to return to one's allegiance. Cf. No. 1262.
933 隆 — *lung*², glorious.
934 薩 — *sa*¹,⁴, P'u-*sa*.

935 吝 — *lin*⁴, stingy.
936 紊 — *wên*⁴, confusion.
937 蚉 — *wên*², a mosquito. Commonly written 蚊.
938 奴 — *nu*², a slave.
939 如 — *ju*¹,², if; as.
940 孥 — *nu*², one's children or grand-children.
941 拏 — *na*², to grasp.
942 帑 — *t'ang*³, a treasury.
943 努 — *nu*³, effort.
944 弩 — *nu*³, a cross-bow.
945 絮 — *hsü*⁴, verbosity; tautology, gossamer.

| 946 | 恕 | — shu⁴, to pardon.
| 947 | 怒 | — nu⁴, anger.
| 948 | 怨 | — yüan⁴, resentment.

| 949 | 際 | — chi⁴, a limit; a point of time. See No. 501.
| 950 | 隙 | — hsi⁴, a crevice. *From* 祭 *Chi⁴, a meat offering.*

| 951 | 腎 | — shên⁴, the kidneys.
| 952 | 賢 | — hsien², virtuous. *Conf.* 監 *Chien = to superintend, a prison,*

| 953 | 啟 | — ch'i³, to begin; to state.
| 954 | 辟 | — p'i³, punishment; to kill. Whence:—
| 955 | 劈 | — p'i¹, to break open. Read p'i³, firewood.
| 956 | 擘 | — p'i³, the thumb; *fig.*, very good.
| 957 | 臂 | — pei⁴, the arm.
| 958 | 壁 | — pi³, a wall.
| 959 | 璧 | — pi⁴, a valuable stone; to decline.
| 960 | 譬 | — p'i⁴, for instance.
| 961 | 避 | — pi⁴, to get out of the way.

IN CHINESE CHARACTER.   69

962 单 or 單 — *tan*¹, single; a list; a bill.

963 卑 — *pei*¹, inferior.

---

964 夏 — *hsia*⁴, summer. *cf.* 寡 *kua*³ = lone, few.

965 憂 — *yu*¹, grief. Hence 優 *yu*¹, ease,
            and 擾 *jao*³, to give trouble.

---

966 己 — *chi*³, oneself. The 6th of the Ten Stems. Hence

967 巳 — *i*³, already. Hence 圯 *i*³, a bridge

968 巳 — *ssŭ*⁴, 9 to 11 a.m. The 6th of the Twelve Branches

---

969 勺 — *shao*², a spoon. Hence 約 *yo*¹, a treaty.

970 勻 — *yün*², equal. Hence 均 *chün*¹, all.

971 勾 — *kou*¹, to hook on.

972 句 — *chü*⁴, a sentence. Hence 苟 *kou*³, if;
                            狗 *kou*³, a dog;
               and 拘 *chü*¹, to grasp.

973 旬 — *hsün*², a period of ten days.

974 匈 — *hsiung*¹, the breast. Same as 胸.

975 包 — *pao*¹, to wrap. See No. 1223.

976 釣 — tiao⁴, to angle.
977 鈞 — chün¹, thirty catties; important.
978 鉤 — kou¹, a hook.

---

979 可 — k'o¹·²·³, can.
980 司 — ssŭ¹, to manage. *A township.*
981 何 — ho², how? what? who?
982 伺 — tz'ŭ⁴, to attend upon.

---

983 同 — t'ung², with. Hence 筒 t'ung³, a tube.
984 向 — hsiang⁴, towards.

---

985 踏 — ta⁴, to beat time with the foot; to trample.
986 蹈 — tao⁴, to tread in the footsteps of.
    From 舀 yao³, to bale out.
    So 稻 tao⁴, paddy. *& 掏 tāo¹ = to pull*

---

987 招 — ch'ia¹, to cull, *nip between finger + thumb. Cf. 拮*
988 諂 — ch'an³, to flatter.   } *From 臽*
989 餡 — hsien⁴, stuffing.   } *Hsien + = a pit* *to follow / lay hold*

IN CHINESE CHARACTER.   71

990 陷 — *hsien*⁴, to fall into.

991 險 — *hsien*³, dangerous. From 僉 *ch'ien*¹, all.

992 斂 — *lien*⁴, to collect.

993 劍 or 劒 — *chien*⁴, a sword.

994 簽 — *ch'ien*¹, lots for drawing; to subscribe. *to write*

995 臉 — *lien*³, the face.

996 檢 — *chien*³, to take an account of.

997 儉 — *chien*³,⁴, economical.

998 殮 — *lien*⁴, to dress a corpse for burial.

———

999 去 — *ch'ü*⁴, to go.

1000 丟 — *tiu*¹, to lose.

———

1001 却 — *ch'üeh*⁴, a particle; to refuse.

1002 刦 or 刧 — *chieh*², to steal.

———

郄 — *ch'üeh*⁴, same as 却 above.

1003 欲 — *yü*⁴, to desire.

1004 老 — *lao³*, old.

1005 考 — *k'ao³*, to examine.

1006 孝 — *hsiao⁴*, filial. Hence 教 *chiao¹·⁴*, to teach.

1007 暑 — *shu³*, heat.

1008 署 — *shu³·⁴*, a yamên; acting for.

1009 貧 — *p'in²*, poor.

1010 貪 — *t'an¹*, to covet.

1011 賚 — *lai⁴*, to bestow.

1012 賫 or 齎 — *chi¹*, to deliver up.

1013 誘 — *yu⁴*, to mislead.

1014 諉 — *wei³*, to excuse oneself.

1015 誨 — *hui³*, to instruct; to induce.

1016 詭 — *kuei³*, strange; to calumniate.

1017 諱 — *hui⁴*, to dread; to make a reservation.

IN CHINESE CHARACTER.   73

1018 雨 — *yü³*, rain.
1019 兩 — *liang¹·³*, two; an ounce.

1020 扇 — *shan⁴*, a fan.
1021 漏 — *lou⁴*, to leak. Cf. 滬 Hu⁴ = to fish with stakes; Shanghai.
1022 滿 — *man³*, full.

1023 從 — *tsung⁴*, family; followers. *ts'ung⁴*, from; by; to comply. orig. form 从
1024 徙 — *hsi¹·³*, to change one's abode.
1025 徒 辻 — *t'u²*, a disciple; an apprentice; foot soldier, ruffian; in

1026 陡 — *tou³*, suddenly.
1027 陟 — *chih²*, to advance.

1028 駛 — *shih³*, to move quickly.
1029 馳 — *ch'ih²*, to go full speed.

1030 找 — *chao³*, to seek.
1031 我 — *wo³*, I; me.

1032 羔 — *kao*¹, a lamb. So 糕 *kao*¹, cake.
1033 恙 — *yang*⁴, disease.
1034 美 — *mei*³, handsome.
1035 羌 — *ch'iang*¹, western shepherds; barbarians.
1036 姜 — *chiang*¹, name of a river; a surname.

1037 養 — *yang*³, to nourish.
1038 義 — *i*⁴, right; moral &c.
1039 羲 — *hsi*⁴, a surname.

1040 埋 — *mai*², to bury.
1041 理 — *li*³, principle.

1042 擊 — *chi*¹·⁴, to strike.
1043 繫 — *hsi*⁴, to bind.

1044 選 — *hsüan*³, to choose.
1045 遣 — *ch'ien*¹, to remove; to drive away.

1046 頂 — *ting³*, the top.
1047 項 — *hsiang⁴*, kind; sort.

1048 具 — *chü⁴*, to prepare. Hence 俱 *chü¹·⁴*, all.
1049 貝 — *pei⁴*, precious.
1050 且 — *ch'ieh³*, moreover. Hence 宜 *i¹·²·³*, ought; right.

1051 朕 — *chên⁴*, the Imperial WE.
1052 脫 — *t'o¹·³*, to take off. From 兌 *tui⁴*, to weigh.

1053 稅 — *shui⁴*, taxes.
1054 租 — *tsu¹*, to rent. So:—

1055 姐 — *chieh³*, an elder sister.
1056 祖 — *tsu³*, ancestors.
1057 粗 or 麤 — *ts'u¹*, coarse.
1058 阻 — *tsu³*, to stop; to hinder.

1059 密 — *mi⁴*, secret.
1060 蜜 — *mi⁴*, honey. = 蜜 honey, fr. 宓 Phonetic

1061 螽 — *chung¹*, a kind of locust; prolific.
1062 蠭 — *fêng¹*, a bee. Also written 蜂.

1063 省 — *shêng³*, a province; to save. Read *hsing³*, to think.
1064 雀 — *ch'iao³*, small birds.

1065 迄 — *hsi³*, until.
1066 迤 — *i²*, towards.

1067 洋 — *yang²*, the ocean; foreign.
1068 津 — *chin¹* or *ching¹*, a ford.

1069 奥 — *ao⁴*, abstruse; Austro-Hungarian.
1070 粤 — *yüeh⁴*, the two *Kuang* provinces.

1071 問 — *wên*⁴, to ask.
1072 間 — *chien*⁴, numerative of rooms &c.
1073 聞 — *wên*², to hear.
1074 閒 — *hsien*², leisure; idle.
1075 閑 — *hsien*², to obstruct. *Cf.* 閉 *Pi* = shut up, seclude

1076 牆 — *ch'iang*², a wall. From 嗇 *sê*¹, stingy.
1077 牕 — *ch'uang*¹, a window. Correctly written 窗.

1078 鍾 — *chung*¹, a cup. See No. 549.
1079 鐘 — *chung*¹, a bell. See No. 1175.
1080 鏡 — *ching*⁴, a mirror.

1081 甚 — *shên*²·⁴, very; what?
1082 其 — *ch'i*², he; she; it &c.

1083 斯 — *ssŭ*¹, this; that.
1084 欺 — *ch'i*¹, to deceive.
1085 期 — *ch'i*², a period of time; to hope.

1086 斟 — *chên*¹·³, to pour out; to deliberate.
1087 勘 — *k'an*⁴, personal investigation.

1088 湛 — *chan*⁴, glossy.
1089 堪 — *k'an*¹, to be worthy of.

1090 酸 — *suan*¹, sour.
1091 醋 — *ts'u*⁴, vinegar.
1092 醉 — *tsui*⁴, drunk.

1093 乾 — *kan*¹, dry. *Ch'ien*¹, of Emperor Ch'ien Lung.
1094 幹 — *kan*⁴, to transact business.

1095 翰 — *han*², a pencil; the *Han*-lin-yüan.
1096 韓 — *han*², a surname.

1097 辨 — *pien*⁴, to distinguish between.
1098 辦 — *pan*⁴, to transact business.
1099 辯 — *pien*⁴, to argue.

[Continued—

Continued—

1100 辮 — *pien⁴*, to plait.

1101 瓣 — *p'an¹* or *pan⁴*, petals.

1102 施 — *shih¹*, to set.

1103 旂 — *ch'i²*, a flag. Commonly written 旗.

1104 旅 — *lü³*, traders.

1105 旌 — *ching¹*, a distinction; a banner.

1106 族 — *tsu²*, a clan; a family.

1107 旋 — *hsüan¹·²*, to turn round; by and by. *Chou'-hsüa* = to treat fri[endly]

1108 旄 — *mao²*, part of a banner.

1109 奇 — *ch'i²*, odd; strange.

1110 寄 — *chi⁴*, a letter.

寄
定

1111 祠 — *ssŭ²*, to sacrifice to one's ancestors.

1112 社 — *shê⁴*, the *Genius loci*.

1113 祀 — *ssŭ⁴*, to sacrifice.

1114 祈 — *ch'i²*, to hope.

[Continued—

Continued—

1115 祝 — *chu*²,⁴, blessings; to pray.
1116 祐 — *yu*⁴, divine protection.
1117 祜 — *hu*⁴, happiness.

1118 逐 — *chu*², to expel; seriatim.
1119 遂 — *sui*¹,², to accord with; to yield.

1120 墮 — *to*⁴, to fall down. *Also written* 隨 *or* 隳 to break
1121 墜 — *chui*⁴, to hang down.

1122 巴 — *pa*¹, 巴不得 would that! See No. 1170.
1123 色 — *sê*⁴, colour; sensuality.
1124 邑 — *yi*⁴, a hamlet.

1125 攝 — *shê*⁴, to direct; to control.
1126 撬 — *ch'iao*⁴, to prise open.

1127 詢 — *hsün*², to enquire about.
1128 訊 — *hsün*⁴, to examine *judicially*.
1129 訓 — *hsün*⁴, to teach.

1130 堅 — chien¹, to establish.

1131 竪 — shu⁴, perpendicular.

1132 豎 — shu⁴, a child. [Same as above.]

1133 緊 — chin³, important. 緊

1134 監 — chien¹, to oversee; a eunuch.
Hence 藍 lan², blue;
鑑 chien⁴, a mirror.

1135 檻 — k'an³, a threshold.

1136 欖 — lan³, the olive.

1137 翌 — i⁴, tomorrow.

1138 習 — hsi¹,², to practise.

1139 翟 — chai² or ti², a surname.

1140 瞿 — ch'ü², a surname. Hence 懼 chü⁴, to fear.

1141 戮 — lu⁴, to kill.

1142 戳 — ch'uo¹, a seal.

1143 勞 — *lao²*, trouble; merit.

1144 榮 — *jung²* or *yung²*, honour; rank. Cf. 縈 *Yin* = to coil round, embarrass.

1145 螢 — *ying²* or *yung²*, the glow-worm.

1146 營 — *ying²*, a camp.

1147 塋 — *ying²*, a grave.

1148 瑩 — *ying²* or *yung²*, bright; lustrous.

1149 熒 — *ying²* or *yung²*, fiery; luminous.

1150 樂 — *lê⁴*, mirth. Read *yo⁴*, music.

1151 藥 — *yao⁴*, medicine.

1152 彎 — *wan¹*, to bend. Hence 灣 *wan¹*, a bay.

1153 變 — *pien⁴*, to change.

1154 戀 — *lien⁴* or *lüan⁴*, attachment to. 攣

1155 鑾 — *luan²*, bells on the Imperial carriage.

1156 蠻 — *man²*, barbarous tribes of the south.

1157 丘 — *ch'iu¹*, a mound; a tumulus.

1158 兵 — *ping¹*, a soldier.

1159 岳 — *yo⁴*, father or mother-*in-law*.

1160 母 — *mu³*, mother. Hence 每 *mei³*, every.

1161 毋 — *wu²·⁴*, a prohibitive particle.

1162 屢 — *lü³*, often.

1163 履 — *li³*, to tread; antecedents.

1164 片 — *p'ien⁴*, a slice.

1165 爿 — *ch'uang²*, a bed. Read *p'an²*, numerative of 店 *tien*.

1166 曾 — *tsêng¹* or *ts'êng²*, a sign of the past tense.

1167 會 — *hui³·⁴*, to meet together; a guild.

1168 紂 — *chou⁴*, last prince of the Shang dynasty.

1169 糾 — *chiu¹·³*, to collect together.

1170 肥 — *fei²*, fat. See No. 1122.

1171 肺 — *fei⁴*, the lungs. See No. 569.

1172 瑞 — *jui⁴*, a good omen.

1173 端 — *tuan¹*, correct. So 揣 *ch'uai¹·³*, to guess.

1174 畜 — *ch'u⁴*, a brute. Hence 蓄 *hsü⁴*, to store.

1175 童 — *t'ung²*, a boy. See No. 1079.

1176 乜 — *mieh²*, to squint.

1177 也 — *yeh³*, also; even then &c.

1178 世 — *shih²,⁴*, a generation.

1179 池 — *ch'ih²*, a pond.

1180 泄 — *hsieh⁴*, dysentery.

1181 勿 — *wu⁴*, do not. Hence 刎 *wên³*, to cut one's throat.

1182 匆 or 怱 — *ts'ung¹*, hurry.

1183 忽 — *hu¹*, suddenly. See No. 1077.

1184 料 — *liao²,⁴*, to calculate.

1185 科 — *k'o¹*, class; rank; examinations.

1186 鄉 — *hsiang¹*, a village; a neighbourhood.

1187 卿 — *ch'ing¹*, a title of high officials.

1188 凡 — chi¹·³, a stool. Hence 飢 chi¹, famine.
1189 凡 — fan²·³, all. Hence 帆 fan¹, a sail.
1190 九 — chiu³, nine.
1191 丸 — wan², pills.

1192 喝 — ho¹·⁴, to drink. *to shout to, call; scold*.
1193 渴 — k'o³, thirsty.
1194 揭 — chieh¹, a placard; to pull down.
1195 竭 — chieh², to try one's best. *extreme*.
1196 歇 — hsieh¹, to rest.
1197 謁 — yeh⁴, to visit.

1198 訐 — chieh², to investigate judicially.
1199 許 — hsü³, to allow; to betroth. See No. 12.
1200 詐 — cha⁴, treacherous. So 作 tso¹·²·⁴, to make; to do. From 乍 cha⁴, suddenly.

1201 號 — hao²·⁴, a name or epithet. From 虎 hu³, a tiger.
1202 跨 — k'ua⁴, to pass over; to sit on.

1203 忠 — *chung¹*, loyal.

1204 患 — *huan⁴*, calamity. From 串 *ch'uan⁴*, connected.

1205 惠 — *hui⁴*, kindness.

1206 墾 — *k'ên³*, to plough up. See No. 269.

1207 懇 — *k'ên³*, to implore.

1208 棄 — *ch'i⁴*, to reject. or 棄

1209 葉 — *yeh⁴*, leaves. from 枽 Yeh⁴ = a leaf, flat piece

1210 局 — *chü⁴*, an office; a square on a chess-board.

1211 居 — *chü¹*, to dwell.

1212 屆 — *chieh⁴*, a point of time.

1213 屈 — *ch'ü¹*, a grievance.

1214 戾 — *li⁴*, unruly. Hence 淚 *lei⁴*, tears.

1215 亞 — *a* or *ya³,⁴*, second.

1216 惡 — *ê⁴* or *wu⁴*, bad; wicked.

1217 壺 — hu^2, a pot.
1218 壼 — $k'un^{1.3}$, women's apartments.

1219 役 — yi^4, a servant.
1220 投 — $t'ou^2$, to hit the mark; to jump into.
1221 設 — $shê^4$, to set up; to devise.

1222 跪 — $kuei^4$, to kneel. From 危 $wei^{2.3}$, dangerous.
1223 跑 — $p'ao^3$, to run. See No. 975.

1224 斤 — $chin^1$, a pound; a catty.
1225 斥 — $ch'ih^4$, to drive away; to scold. Chik-kê = to deprive of rank, to dismiss.

1226 折 — $chê^2$ or $shê^2$, to break.
1227 拆 — $ch'ai^1$, to pull down, rip open (as a letter), pull

---

1228 訢 — $hsin^1$, joyful; part of Prince Kung's name. Same as 欣.
1229 訴 — su^4, to tell; to accuse.

1230 乃 — *nai*³, on the contrary &c.　仍 *jêng*²·³, as before;
　　　　　　　　　　　　　　　扔 *jêng*¹·³, to throw.
1231 及 — *chi*², to extend to; together with.　See No. 644.

1232 銷 — *hsiao*¹, to dissolve; to finish; to cancel.
1233 鎖 or 鏁 — *so*³, a lock.

1234 突 — *t'u*¹ or *tu*⁴, suddenly.
1235 究 — *chiu*¹, to investigate.

1236 今 — *chin*¹, now.
1237 令 — *ling*⁴, orders.

1238 遽 — *chü*⁴, hurriedly. So 劇 *chi*⁴, distressing; ⎫ From
　　　　　　　　　　　　　　　　　　據 *chü*⁴, according to. ⎭
1239 遞 — *ti*⁴, to hand; transmit.　From 虍 *Sŭ*¹ = a horned tiger.

1240 瑟 — *sê*¹, a stringed instrument.
1241 琵 — *p'i*², a guitar.

1242 毃 — *ku³*, a cart-wheel.
1243 穀 — *kou⁴*, enough; to reach.
1244 穀 — *ku¹*, grain. *conf.* 榖 *Ku³* = the paper mulberry
1245 毅 — *i⁴*, fortitude.

1246 咒 — *chou⁴*, to curse. *gibberish prayers, for rain etc.*
1247 哭 — *k'u¹*, to weep.

1248 呂 — *lü³*, Spain; Manila.
1249 宮 — *kung¹*, a palace.

1250 刮 — *kua¹*, to scrape.
1251 刷 — *shua¹*, to brush.

1252 腦 — *nao³*, brains. So 惱 *nao³*, to get angry.
1253 臘 — *la⁴*, the 12th moon.
    Wrongly used for 蠟 *la⁴*, a candle.
    So 獵 *lieh⁴*, to hunt.

1254 辭 — *tz'ŭ²*, to decline; to dismiss.
1255 亂 — *lan⁴* or *luan⁴*, confusion.

1256 挂 — *kua⁴*, to hang up.

1257 桂 — *kuei⁴*, the cinnamon tree.

1258 卦 — *kua⁴*, divination.

1259 封 — *fêng¹*, to seal.

1260 拈 — *nien¹,²*, to take with the fingers. See No. 1272.

1261 捏 — *nieh¹*, to make up false reports.

1262 逢 — *fêng²*, to meet. Hence 縫 *fêng⁴*, to sew. *From 夆 Fêng¹: mutual opposition; to meet. See No.*

1263 篷 — *p'êng²*, a sail.

1264 蓬 — *p'êng²*, a plant; luxuriant.

1265 寅 — *yen²*, 3 to 5 p.m. *or yin. The 3rd of the Twelve Branches*

1266 夤 — *yen²*, bribery. *of 宙 Chóu⁴ = to hold as th all ages: from remote an*

1267 演 — *yen³*, to practise.

1268 駱 — *lo⁴*, the camel.

1269 駝 — *t'o²*, the camel.

1270 馱 — *to⁴*, a burden. Read *t'o²*, to support.

1271 古 — *ku¹*, ancient. Hence 故 *ku⁴*, because.

1272 占 — *chan¹˙⁴*, to divine. Hence:—

1273 佔 — *chan⁴*, to encroach.

1274 沾 — *chan¹˙³*, to be steeped in.

1275 拈 — *nien¹˙²*, to take with the fingers.

1276 毡 — *chan¹*, felt. Same as 氈.

1277 玷 — *tien⁴*, blemish; to disgrace.

1278 站 — *chan⁴*, to stand up.

1279 帖 — *t'ieh¹˙³˙⁴*, a placard; a scroll.

1280 貼 — *t'ieh¹˙⁴*, to paste; attached to.

1281 粘 — *chan¹* or *nien²*, to stick; to paste.

1282 黏 — *nien²*, sticky. Same as preceding. See also No. 635.

1283 菱 — *chien¹*, a few.

1284 箋 — *chien¹*, note-paper. Also written 牋.

1285 盞 — *chan³*, numerative of lamps.

1286 淺 — *ch'ien³*, shallow.

[Continued—

SYNOPTICAL STUDIES

Continued—

1287 棧 — *chan⁴*, warehouse; godown.
1288 錢 — *ch'ien²*, money.
1289 賤 — *chien⁴*, cheap.
1290 踐 — *chien⁴*, to tread upon.
1291 殘 — *ts'an²*, in ruins; faded.

1292 高 — *kao¹*, high.
1293 嵩 — *sung¹*, a surname.
1294 蒿 — *hao¹*, a kind of plant.
1295 篙 — *kao¹*, a punt-pole.

1296 毫 — *hao²*, a hair; a tittle. a ten-cent piece. Cf. 毫
1297 膏 — *kao¹*, rich food; sticking-plaster.
1298 槀 — *kao³*, a rough draught. Same as 稿.
1299 豪 — *hao²*, eminent; a hero. Domineering..

1300 橋 — *ch'iao²*, a bridge.
1301 稿 — same as 槀 *kao³*, a rough draught.

1302 易 — i⁴, to change; easy. So 錫 hsi¹·², zinc;
1303 昜 — yang², the sun.   賜 tz'ŭ⁴, to bestow;
                              剔 t'i¹, to pick out;
                              踢 t'i¹, to kick.

1304 場 — ch'ang²·³, an arena. Same as No. 1312.
1305 揚 — yang², to publish.
1306 楊 — yang², arbutus.
                              or 宏 cf. 宏 Hung² great, vast
1307 湯 — t'ang¹, soup. Hence 蕩 tang⁴, to dissipate.
1308 腸 — ch'ang², entrails.
1309 陽 — yang², the sun. Same as No. 1303.
1310 暢 — ch'ang⁴, hilarity. To penetrate, increase.

1311 傷 — shang¹, a wound.
1312 塲 — ch'ang²·³, an arena. Same as No. 1304.
1313 殤 — shang¹, to die.

1314 刻 — k'o¹·³·⁴, to engrave; a ¼ of an hour.
1315 劾 — ho², to accuse to the Emperor.
1316 該 — kai¹, to owe.
1317 亥 — hai, the 12th of the Twelve Branches.

6

INDEX.

a	...	亞	No. 1215	Continued—			
ai	...	呆	,, 186	chan	...	占	No. 1272
,,	...	愛	,, 441	,,	...	佔	,, 1273
,,	...	哀	,, 758	,,	...	沾	,, 1274
,,	...	矮	,, 674	,,	...	氈	,, 1276
an	...	岸	,, 117	,,	...	站	,, 1278
ang	...	昂	,, 297	,,	...	粘	,, 1281
ao	...	傲	,, 850	ch'an	...	廛	,, 370
,,	...	奧	,, 1069	,,	...	纏	,, 370
cha	...	詐	,, 1200	,,	...	諂	,, 988
,,	...	乍	,, 1200	chang	...	丈	,, 390
ch'a	...	查	,, 184	,,	...	長	,, 307
,,	...	茶	,, 206	,,	...	掌	,, 129
,,	...	詫	,, 246	ch'ang	...	昌	,, 90
,,	...	答	,, 502	,,	...	嘗	,, 137
,,	...	叉	,, 110	,,	...	常	,, 133
,,	...	察	,, 501	,,	...	償	,, 136
chai	...	宅	,, 242	,,	...	敞	,, 924
,,	...	寨	,, 530	,,	...	揚	,, 1304
,,	...	債	,, 894	,,	...	場	,, 1312
,,	...	摘	,, 920	,,	...	腸	,, 1308
,,	...	翟	,, 1139	,,	...	唱	,, 90
ch'ai	...	柴	,, 228	,,	...	暢	,, 1310
,,	...	拆	,, 1227	chao	...	爪	,, 112
,,	...	差	,, 59	,,	...	叉	,, 111
chan	...	貶	,, 730	,,	...	找	,, 1030
,,	...	湛	,, 1088	,,	...	沼	,, 365
,,	...	盞	,, 1285	chê	...	遮	,, 354
,,	...	棧	,, 1287	,,	...	折	,, 1226
			[Continued—	,,	...	輒	,, 855

				Continued—			
ch'ê	...	撒	No. 855	chi	...	集	No. 752
,,	...	徹	,, 848	,,	...	籍	,, 782
chên	...	鍼 or 針	,, 321	,,	...	激	,, 845
,,	...	臻	,, 486	,,	...	績	,, 896
,,	...	陣	,, 726	,,	...	積	,, 897
,,	...	酖	,, 1086	,,	...	稽	,, 898
,,	...	朕	,, 1051	,,	...	際	,, 949
ch'ên	...	臣	,, 806	,,	...	已	,, 966
,,	...	辰	,, 306	,,	...	霽	,, 1012
,,	...	陳	,, 727	,,	...	罄	,, 1042
,,	...	塵	,, 371	,,	...	寄	,, 1110
chêng	...	徵	,, 851	,,	...	几	,, 1188
,,	...	鄭	,, 600	,,	...	及	,, 1231
ch'êng	...	呈	,, 833	,,	...	繼	,, 653
,,	...	掙	,, 130	,,	...	極	,, 156
,,	...	懲 or 徵	,, 854	,,	...	爵	,, 667
,,	...	丞 or 承	,, 157	,,	...	羈	,, 668
chi	...	冀	,, 171	,,	...	飢	,, 1188
,,	...	亟	,, 156	,,	...	劇	,, 1238
,,	...	棘	,, 239	ch'i	...	漆	,, 222
,,	...	季	,, 216	,,	...	戚	,, 310
,,	...	戟	,, 344	,,	...	緝	,, 915
,,	...	即	,, 288	,,	...	啓	,, 953
,,	...	既	,, 291	,,	...	旂	,, 1103
,,	...	暨	,, 291	,,	...	奇	,, 1109
,,	...	祭	,, 501	,,	...	祈	,, 1114
,,	...	基	,, 526	,,	...	欺	,, 1084
,,	...	脊	,, 480	,,	...	期	,, 1085
,,	...	紀	,, 643	,,	...	棄	,, 1208
,,	...	級	,, 644	,,	...	其	,, 1082
			[Continued—	,,	...	柒	,, 201

INDEX.

				Continued—			
chia	...	佳	No. 748	chich	...	藉	No. 781
,,	...	嘉	,, 778	,,	...	階	,, 929
,,	...	叚	,, 840	,,	...	刦 or 刼	,, 1002
,,	...	假	,, 840	,,	...	姐	,, 1055
,,	...	夾	,, 733	,,	...	揭	,, 1194
,,	...	挾	,, 737	,,	...	竭	,, 1195
,,	...	價	,, 866	,,	...	訐	,, 1198
ch'ia	...	恰	,, 710	,,	...	屆	,, 1212
,,	...	揩	,, 987	,,	...	節	,, 292
chiang	...	港	,, 488	,,	...	捷	,, 589
,,	...	降	,, 932	,,	...	觧 or 解	,, 858
,,	...	彊	,, 655	ch'ieh	...	怯	,, 708
,,	...	疆	,, 656	,,	...	且	,, 1050
,,	...	姜	,, 1036	,,	...	妾	,, 61
ch'iang	...	戕	,, 335	chien	...	肩	,, 145
,,	...	牆	,, 1076	,,	...	減	,, 322
,,	...	羌	,, 1035	,,	...	漸	,, 323
chiao	...	焦	,, 751	,,	...	建	,, 349
,,	...	繳	,, 846	,,	...	健	,, 432
,,	...	徼	,, 849	,,	...	薦	,, 531
,,	...	狡	,, 736	,,	...	賤	,, 1289
,,	...	交	,, 732	,,	...	踐	,, 1290
,,	...	絞	,, 736	,,	...	揀	,, 722
,,	...	郊	,, 740	,,	...	劍	,, 993
,,	...	敎	,, 1006	,,	...	檢	,, 996
ch'iao	...	橋	,, 1300	,,	...	儉	,, 997
,,	...	雀	,, 1064	,,	...	間	,, 1072
,,	...	撬	,, 1126	,,	...	堅	,, 1130
chich	...	皆	,, 282	,,	...	鑑 監	,, 1134
,,	...	界	,, 168	,,	...	兼	,, 542
				,,	...	艱	,, 533
			[Continued—				[Continued—

INDEX.

Continued—				Continued—			
chien	...	諫	No. 725	*ch'ih*	...	馳	No. 1029
,,	...	尖	,, 1283	,,	...	池	,, 1179
,,	...	簽 or 牋	,, 1284	,,	...	掣	,, 803
,,	...	柬	,, 721	,,	...	斥	,, 1225
,,	...	菅	,, 809	*chin*	...	金	,, 691
,,	...	鑑	,, 1134	,,	...	錦	,, 303
ch'ien	...	千	,, 19	,,	...	進	,, 63
,,	...	遣	,, 910	,,	...	近	,, 64
,,	...	遷	,, 1045	,,	...	盡	,, 597
,,	...	謙	,, 546	,,	...	儘	,, 598
,,	...	黔	,, 634	,,	...	僅	,, 599
,,	...	淺	,, 1286	,,	...	覲	,, 514
,,	...	錢	,, 1288	,,	...	晉	,, 358
,,	...	歉	,, 548	,,	...	禁	,, 377
,,	...	僉	,, 991	,,	...	津	,, 1068
,,	...	簽	,, 994	,,	...	筋	,, 293
chih	...	紙	,, 263	,,	...	緊	,, 1133
,,	...	炙	,, 373	,,	...	今	,, 1236
,,	...	治	,, 700	,,	...	斤	,, 1224
,,	...	執	,, 466	,,	...	衿	,, 714
,,	...	陟	,, 1027	*ch'in*	...	秦	,, 486
,,	...	之	,, 728	,,	...	勤	,, 512
,,	...	擲	,, 600	,,	...	親	,, 515
,,	...	製	,, 802	,,	...	衾	,, 713
,,	...	制	,, 802	*ching*	...	精	,, 879
ch'ih	...	尺	,, 31	,,	...	靜	,, 877
,,	...	勅 or 敕	,, 238	,,	...	井	,, 793
,,	...	持	,, 251	,,	...	淨	,, 862
,,	...	笞	,, 703	,,	...	鏡	,, 1080
,,	...	飭	,, 459	,,	...	旌	,, 1105
,,	...	赤	,, 477	,,	...	靖	,, 872
		[Continued—		,,	...	睛	,, 876

INDEX.

ch'ing	...	青	No.	870	Continued—		
,,	...	清	,,	871	,,	... 局	No. 1210
,,	...	情	,,	874	,,	... 居	,, 1211
,,	...	晴	,,	875	,,	... 巨	,, 805
,,	...	請	,,	878	,,	... 拒	,, 813
,,	...	卿	,,	1187	,,	... 矩	,, 816
chiu	...	九	,,	1190	,,	... 鉅	,, 815
,,	...	究	,,	1235	,,	... 距	,, 814
,,	...	久	,,	67	,,	... 具	,, 1048
,,	...	灸	,,	374	,,	... 俱	,, 1048
,,	...	舅	,,	177	,,	... 懼	,, 1140
,,	...	舊	,,	181	,,	... 遽	,, 1238
,,	...	酒	,,	102	,,	... 舉	,, 89
,,	...	糾	,,	1169	ch'ü	... 曲	,, 84
ch'iu	...	丘	,,	1157	,,	... 區	,, 811
,,	...	秋	,,	665	,,	... 去	,, 999
,,	...	求	,,	44	,,	... 驅	,, 1140
,,	...	囚	,,	122	,,	... 屈	,, 1213
cho	...	捉	,,	587	chüan	... 卷	,, 489
chou	...	舟	,,	788	,,	... 捲	,, 489
,,	...	胄	,,	93	,,	... 倦	,, 489
,,	...	州	,,	42	,,	... 眷	,, 481
,,	...	晝	,,	595	,,	... 捐	,, 911
,,	...	紂	,,	1168	,,	... 絹	,, 914
,,	...	咒	,,	1246	ch'üan	... 犬	,, 5
ch'ou	...	紬	,,	80	,,	... 泉	,, 302
,,	...	抽	,,	77	,,	... 拳	,, 490
,,	...	臭	,,	189	,,	... 全	,, 491
chü	...	句	,,	972	,,	... 勸	,, 690
,,	...	拘	,,	972	,,	... 權	,, 902
					,,	... 圈	,, 906
			[Continued—		,,		,, 489

INDEX.

chŭeh	...	決	No. 49	chui	...	追	No. 280
ch'ŭeh	...	却 or 郄	,, 1001	,,	...	隹	,, 749
,,	...	缺	,, 53	,,	...	墜	,, 1121
chŭn	...	軍	,, 419	ch'ui	...	垂	,, 538
,,	...	鈞	,, 977	chun	...	准	,, 715
,,	...	均	,, 970	,,	...	準	,, 717
chu	...	諸	,, 593	ch'un	...	唇	,, 309
,,	...	住	,, 745	,,	...	春	,, 482
,,	...	筯	,, 294	,,	...	椿	,, 492
,,	...	祝	,, 1115	chung	...	重	,, 549
,,	...	逐	,, 1118	,,	...	鍾	,, 1078
,,	...	麆	,, 372	,,	...	鐘	,, 1079
ch'u	...	楚	,, 378	,,	...	衷	,, 759
,,	...	除	,, 553	,,	...	螽	,, 1061
,,	...	齊	,, 1174	,,	...	忠	,, 1203
ch'uai	...	揣	,, 1173	ch'ung	...	充	,, 70
chuan	...	轉	,, 418	,,	...	舂	,, 483
,,	...	専	,, 399	,,	...	崇	,, 561
ch'uan	...	穿	,, 131	ch'uo	...	悇	,, 707
,,	...	傳	,, 399	,,	...	㺄	,, 1142
,,	...	船	,, 789	ê ...	...	惡	,, 1216
,,	...	川	,, 41	ên...	...	恩	,, 125
,,	...	串	,, 1204	fa	...	發	,, 505
chuang	...	樁	,, 493	,,	...	伐	,, 676
,,	...	壯	,, 333	,,	...	乏	,, 729
,,	...	狀	,, 334	fan	...	反	,, 570
,,	...	莊	,, 333	,,	...	泛	,, 729
,,	...	庄	,, 339	,,	...	番	,, 604
ch'uang	...	床	,, 340	,,	...	蕃	,, 645
,,	...	牀	,, 332	,,	...	潘	,, 608
,,	...	愴	,, 1077	,,	...	籓	,, 609
,,	...	刅	,, 1165			[Continued—	

INDEX.

Continued—

fan	... 橘	No.	611
,,	... 凡	,,	1189
,,	... 焚	,,	380
,,	... 翻	,,	613
,,	... 帆	,,	1189
fang	... 仿	,,	328
,,	... 彷	,,	829
fei	... 市	,,	569
,,	... 肺 569	,,	1171
,,	... 肥	,,	1170
fên	... 奮	,,	180
,,	... 焚	,,	376
fêng	... 奉	,,	484
,,	... 馮	,,	756
,,	... 封	,,	1259
,,	... 逢	,,	1262
,,	... 螽	,,	1062
fo	... 佛	,,	826
fu	... 賦	,,	262
,,	... 浮	,,	861
,,	... 服	,,	792
,,	... 弗	,,	819
,,	... 彿	,,	827
,,	... 復	,,	669
,,	... 覆	,,	670
,,	... 伏	,,	677
,,	... 付	,,	678
,,	... 符	,,	678
,,	... 傅傳	,,	400
,,	... 縛	,,	403
,,	... 賻	,,	405

[Continued—

Continued—

fu	... 夫	No.	7
,,	... 富	,,	139
,,	... 戌	,,	257
,,	... 甫	,,	400
,,	... 府	,,	678
han	... 旱	,,	300
,,	... 函	,,	155
,,	... 咸	,,	316
,,	... 喊	,,	319
,,	... 寒	,,	528
,,	... 含	,,	711
,,	... 翰	,,	1095
,,	... 韓	,,	1096
hao	... 荊	,,	478
,,	... 毫	,,	1296
,,	... 豪	,,	1299
,,	... 號	,,	1201
,,	... 嵩	,,	1294
hei	... 黑	,,	140
hên	... 含	,,	711
,,	... 很 or 狠	,,	273
,,	... 恨	,,	274
hêng	... 亨	,,	460
ho	... 合	,,	693
,,	... 何	,,	981
,,	... 刻	,,	1315
,,	... 喝	,,	1192
,, ,	... 賀	,,	636
hou	... 後	,,	444
,,	... 侯	,,	445
,,	... 候	,,	446

INDEX.

hu	... 乎	No.	24
,,	... 護	,,	907
,,	... 忽	,,	1183
,,	... 壺	,,	1217
,,	... 狐	,,	118
,,	... 戶	,,	144
,,	... 祜	,,	1117
hua	... 華	,,	174
,,	... 畫	,,	596
huai	... 淮	,,	716
,,	... 壞	,,	768
huan	... 還	,,	771
,,	... 宦	,,	808
,,	... 歡	,,	903
,,	... 患	,,	1204
huang	... 荒	,,	95
,,	... 皇	,,	834
hui	... 回	,,	158
,,	... 灰	,,	115
,,	... 麾	,,	388
,,	... 揮	,,	422
,,	... 匯	,,	716
,,	... 毀	,,	838
,,	... 徽	,,	853
,,	... 誨	,,	1015
,,	... 諱	,,	1017
,,	... 會	,,	1167
,,	... 惠	,,	1205
hun	... 昏	,,	284
,,	... 昬	,,	283
,,	... 葷	,,	420
,,	... 渾	,,	421
huo	... 或	No.	315
,,	... 惑	,,	317
,,	... 貨	,,	684
,,	... 獲	,,	908
hsi	... 西	,,	99
,,	... 夕	,,	685
,,	... 希	,,	455
,,	... 迄	,,	1065
,,	... 習	,,	1138
,,	... 細	,,	79
,,	... 嚱	,,	1039
,,	... 喜	,,	777
,,	... 檄	,,	847
,,	... 隙	,,	950
,,	... 徙	,,	1024
,,	... 繫	,,	1043
,,	... 息	,,	127
,,	... 悉	,,	128
,,	... 系	,,	435
,,	... 奚	,,	439
,,	... 係	,,	442
,,	... 膝	,,	498
,,	... 錫	,,	1302
hsia	... 洽	,,	701
,,	... 夏	,,	964
,,	... 狹	,,	737
,,	... 暇	,,	840
,,	... 瑕	,,	840
,,	... 遐	,,	840
,,	... 俠	,,	737
hsiang	... 香	,,	185
,,	... 巷	,,	488

[Continued—

INDEX. 103

Continued—				Continued—			
hsiang	...	享	No. 461	hsien	...	險	No. 991
,,	...	襄	,, 766	,,	...	閉	,, 1074
,,	...	降	,, 932	,,	...	閑	,, 1075
,,	...	向	,, 984	,,	...	限	,, 275
,,	...	項	,, 1047	,,	...	涎	,, 348
,,	...	鄉	,, 1186	,,	...	鮮	,, 857
,,	...	相	,, 616	,,	...	餡	,, 989
,,	...	想	,, 617	hsin	...	新	,, 516
,,	...	箱	,, 618	,,	...	薪	,, 516
hsiao	...	孝	,, 1006	,,	...	信	,, 747
,,	...	曉	,, 254	,,	...	辛	,, 772
,,	...	銷	,, 1232	,,	...	訴	,, 1228
,,	...	小	,, 193	,,	...	心	,, 27
,,	...	効	,, 738	hsing	...	杏	,, 182
,,	...	效	,, 739	,,	...	幸	,, 773
,,	...	蕭	,, 629	,,	...	刑	,, 797
,,	...	篠	,, 630	,,	...	形	,, 798
hsieh	...	些	,, 227	,,	...	星	,, 835
,,	...	藝	,, 474	,,	...	省	,, 1063
,,	...	卸	,, 54	,,	...	興	,, 87
,,	...	泄	,, 1180	hsiu	...	袖	,, 81
,,	...	歇	,, 1196	,,	...	秀	,, 218
,,	...	血	,, 30	,,	...	羞	,, 60
,,	...	斜	,, 662	,,	...	休	,, 679
hsien	...	先	,, 9	,,	...	俯	,, 448
,,	...	賢	,, 952	,,	...	修	,, 449
,,	...	線	,, 305	,,	...	繡	,, 631
,,	...	嫌	,, 545	,,	...	鏽	,, 632
,,	...	咸	,, 316	hsiung	...	熊	,, 368
,,	...	絨	,, 320	,,	...	匈	,, 974
,,	...	陷	,, 990	,,	...	兄	,, 65
			[Continued—				[Continued—

INDEX.

Continued—				Continued—			
hsiung	...	雄	No. 615	i	...	巳	No. 967
hsŭ	...	戌	,, 259	,,	...	宜	,, 1050
,,	...	續	,, 883	,,	...	翌	,, 1137
,,	...	絮	,, 945	,,	...	義	,, 1038
,,	...	許	,, 1199	,,	...	縠	,, 1245
,,	...	叙	,, 663	,,	...	疑	,, 672
,,	...	醬	,, 1174	,,	...	易	,, 1302
hsüan	...	玄	,, 433	jan	...	冉	,, 152
,,	...	選	,, 1044	,,	...	染	,, 201
,,	...	旋	,, 1107	jang	...	壤	,, 769
hsün	...	勛 or 勳	,, 519	jao	...	擾	,, 965
,,	...	薰	,, 550	jê	...	熱	,, 468
,,	...	蕭	,, 552	jen	...	壬	,, 830
,,	...	旬	,, 973	,,	...	人	,, 1
,,	...	訽	,, 1127	,,	...	任	,, 744
,,	...	訊	,, 1128	,,	...	刃	,, 196
,,	...	訓	,, 1129	,,	...	忍	,, 196
i	...	巽	,, 169	,,	...	認	,, 196
,,	...	契	,, 172	jêng	...	仍	,, 1230
,,	...	夷	,, 820	,,	...	扔	,, 1230
,,	...	姨	,, 825	jih	...	日	,, 45
,,	...	怡	,, 709	jo	...	若	,, 591
,,	...	貽	,, 704	jou	...	月	,, 786
,,	...	迤	,, 1066	ju	...	入	,, 2
,,	...	遺	,, 909	,,	...	如	,, 939
,,	...	益	,, 350	,,	...	乳	,, 860
,,	...	曳	,, 396	,,	...	辱	,, 308
,,	...	矣	,, 436	jui	...	瑞	,, 1172
,,	...	乂	,, 108	jung	...	絨	,, 264
,,	...	亦	,, 476	,,	...	榮	,, 1144
,,	...	藝	,, 475	,,	...	戎	,, 260
			[Continued—				

INDEX.

kai	... 該	No. 1316	ko	... 戈	No.	256
,,	... 榔	,, 291	,,	... 革	,,	509
k'ai	... 凱	,, 324	,,	... 各	,,	688
,,	... 剴	,, 325	,,	... 格	,,	706
kan	... 感	,, 318	k'o	... 科	,,	1185
,,	... 干	,, 20	,,	... 可	,,	979
,,	... 乾	,, 1093	,,	... 刻	,,	1314
,,	... 幹	,, 1094	,,	... 渴	,,	1193
k'an	... 刊	,, 799	,,	... 克	,,	71
,,	... 勘	,, 1087	,,	... 尅	,,	72
,,	... 坎	,, 1089	kou	... 勾	,,	971
,,	... 檻	,, 1135	,,	... 鈎	,,	978
kang	... 岡	,, 160	,,	... 苟	,,	972
,,	... 綱	,, 162	,,	... 穀	,,	1243
k'ang	... 康	,, 331	,,	... 狗	,,	972
kao	... 杲	,, 187	k'ou	... 寇	,,	74
,,	... 槔	,, 190	ku	... 古	,,	1271
,,	... 高	,, 1292	,,	... 雇	,,	148
,,	... 膏	,, 1297	,,	... 僱	,,	149
,,	... 篙	,, 1395	,,	... 顧	,,	148
,,	... 稿	,, 1301	,,	... 辜	,,	776
,,	... 藁	,, 1298	,,	... 孤	,,	119
,,	... 羔	,, 1032	,,	... 股	,,	791
k'ao	... 考	,, 1005	,,	... 穀	,,	1244
kei	... 給	,, 693	,,	... 賈	,,	866
kên	... 根	,, 276	,,	... 穀	,,	1242
,,	... 跟	,, 278	k'u	... 苦	,,	590
,,	... 艮	,, 269	,,	... 哭	,,	1247
k'ên	... 墾	,, 1206	kua	... 瓜	,,	113
,,	... 懇	,, 1207	,,	... 刮	,,	1250
kêng	... 庚	,, 329	,,	... 挂	,,	1256
,,	... 更	,, 393	,,	... 卦	,,	1258

k'ua	... 跨	No. 1202	kuo	... 國	No.	315
kuai	... 夬	,, 49	,,	... 郭	,,	465
,,	... 乖	,, 536	,,	... 裹	,,	765
,,	... 怪	,, 52	la	... 剌	,,	237
k'uai	... 快	,, 51	,,	... 臘	,,	1253
kuan	... 冠	,, 73	lai	... 來	,,	734
,,	... 官	,, 807	,,	... 賚	,,	1011
,,	... 管	,, 810	lan	... 藍	,,	1134
,,	... 貫	,, 868	,,	... 欖	,,	1136
,,	... 慣	,, 868	,,	... 亂	,,	1255
,,	... 灌	,, 905	,,	... 嬾	,,	379
,,	... 觀	,, 904	lang	... 郎	,,	289
k'uan	... 寬	,, 899	,,	... 朗	,,	290
,,	... 欵	,, 671	,,	... 廊	,,	289
kuei	... 癸	,, 500	,,	... 浪	,,	271
,,	... 貴	,, 867	,,	... 狼	,,	272
,,	... 桂	,, 1257	lao	... 牢	,,	774
,,	... 詭	,, 1016	,,	... 老	,,	1004
,,	... 跪	,, 1222	,,	... 勞	,,	1143
k'uei	... 揆	,, 506	lê	... 樂	,,	1150
kun	... 袞	,, 762	lei	... 雷	,,	164
,,	... 滾	,, 762	,,	... 累	,,	638
k'un	... 昆	,, 281	,,	... 櫐	,,	640
,,	... 困	,, 124	,,	... 壘	,,	641
,,	... 壼	,, 1218	,,	... 淚	,,	1214
,,	... 細	,, 124	li	... 李	,,	215
kung	... 功	,, 647	,,	... 吏	,,	392
,,	... 攻	,, 648	,,	... 裏 or 裡	,,	764
,,	... 宮	,, 1249	,,	... 栗	,,	103
,,	... 躬	,, 660	,,	... 力	,,	199
k'ung	... 孔	,, 859	,,	... 履	,,	1163
,,	... 控	,, 205			[Continued—	

INDEX.

Continued—

li	... 戾	No. 1214	lin	... 淋	No.	682
,,	... 理	,, 1041	,,	... 賃	,,	893
,,	... 梨	,, 224	,,	... 吝	,,	935
,,	... 犂	,, 225	ling	... 陵	,,	931
,,	... 黎	,, 226	,,	... 凌	,,	931
,,	... 曆	,, 356	,,	... 令	,,	1237
,,	... 歷	,, 357	lo	... 勒	,,	511
,,	... 利	,, 426	,,	... 摝	,,	178
,,	... 俐	,, 439	,,	... 駱	,,	1268
,,	... 例	,, 430	lou	... 漏	,,	1021
liang	... 梁	,, 202	lü	... 律	,,	431
,,	... 樑	,, 203	,,	... 呂	,,	1248
,,	... 瓦	,, 267	,,	... 綠	,,	620
,,	... 亮 463	,, 560	,,	... 旅	,,	1104
,,	... 兩	,, 1019	,,	... 屢	,,	1162
liao	... 了	,, 15	,,	... 慮	,,	179
,,	... 料	,, 1184	lüan	... 戀	,,	1154
,,	... 聊	,, 295	lüeh	... 畧	,,	639
lieh	... 列	,, 427	lu	... 祿	,,	621
,,	... 烈	,, 427	,,	... 碌	,,	622
liên	... 歛	,, 992	,,	... 錄	,,	623
,,	... 臉	,, 995	,,	... 陸	,,	930
,,	... 廉	,, 543	,,	... 戮	,,	1141
,,	... 簾	,, 544	,,	... 賂	,,	705
,,	... 鎌	,, 547	luan	... 孿	,,	1155
,,	... 鍊	,, 724	,,	... 亂	,,	1255
,,	... 練	,, 723	,,	... 卵	,,	286
,,	... 聯	,, 296	lun	... 倫	,,	413
,,	... 殓	,, 998	,,	... 論	,,	415
,,	... 連	,, 424	,,	... 輪	,,	417
,,	... 戀	,, 1154	lung	... 隆	,,	933
,,	... 蓮	,, 424				

108　　　　　　INDEX.

ma	... 馬	No. 649	mien	... 綿	No.	304
mai	... 麥	,, 220	,,	... 眠	,,	268
,,	... 埋	,, 1040	,,	... 囬	,,	159
,,	... 買	,, 864	,,	... 面	,,	159
,,	... 賣	,, 865	,,	... 免	,,	312
man	... 蠻	,, 1156	,,	... 勉	,,	314
,,	... 滿	,, 1022	,,	... 棉	,,	304
mang	... 盲	,, 96	min	... 民	,,	266
,,	... 莽	,, 58	,,	... 皿	,,	29
mao	... 毛	,, 23	ming	... 明	,,	33
,,	... 惷	,, 1108	,,	... 名	,,	687
,,	... 昌	,, 91	,,	... 冥	,,	657
,,	... 昴	,, 298	mo	... 末	,,	40
,,	... 卯	,, 285	,,	... 沫 40	,,	681
,,	... 貿	,, 637	,,	... 壘	,,	141
,,	... 貌	,, 651	,,	... 獸	,,	633
,,	... 矛	,, 18	,,	... 麽	,,	385
,,	... 帽	,, 91	,,	... 摩	,,	387
mei	... 眉	,, 146	,,	... 磨	,,	389
,,	... 沒	,, 366	,,	... 莫	,,	508
,,	... 美	,, 1034	,,	... 幕	,,	522
,,	... 妹	,, 39	mu	... 墓	,,	520
mêng	... 夢	,, 55	,,	... 暮	,,	521
mi	... 糜	,, 386	,,	... 慕	,,	523
,,	... 糸	,, 434	,,	... 幕	,,	524
,,	... 密	,, 1059	,,	... 葛	,,	525
,,	... 蜜	,, 1060	,,	... 牧	,,	336
miao	... 藐	,, 652	,,	... 牡	,,	337
mieh	... 滅	,, 311	,,	... 母	,,	1160
,,	... 乜	,, 1176	,,	... 沐	,,	680
			,,	... 木	,,	37

na	... 拏	No.	941	pa	... 八	No.	3
nai	... 奈	,,	555	,,	... 拔	,,	573
,,	... 柰	,,	556	,,	... 巴	,,	1122
,,	... 乃	,,	1230	,,	... 霸	,,	666
nan	... 男	,,	175	pan	... 半	,,	26
,,	... 南	,,	917	,,	... 扳	,,	572
,,	... 難	,,	534	,,	... 般	,,	790
nang	... 囊	,,	767	,,	... 辦	,,	1098
nao	... 腦	,,	1252	,,	... 拌	,,	1101
,,	... 鬧	,,	568	p'an	... 判	,,	800
nêng	... 能	,,	368	,,	... 叛	,,	801
ni	... 逆	,,	210	,,	... 扳	,,	572
,,	... 尼	,,	32	,,	... 潘	,,	607
,,	... 泥	,,	32	,,	... 爿	,,	1165
niang	... 娘	,,	270	pao	... 暴	,,	170
niao	... 鳥	,,	192	,,	... 報	,,	517
nieh	... 臬	,,	188	,,	... 包	,,	975
,,	... 揑	,,	1261	p'ao	... 跑	,,	1223
nien	... 年	,,	14	pei	... 俉 or 俻	,,	450
,,	... 念	,,	712	,,	... 臂	,,	957
,,	... 拈	1260 ,,	1275	,,	... 卑	,,	963
,,	... 粘	,,	1281	,,	... 貝	,,	1049
,,	... 黏	,,	1282	,,	... 倍	,,	363
niu	... 牛	,,	13	,,	... 被	,,	575
no	... 諾	,,	592	p'ei	... 披	,,	574
nu	... 奴	,,	938	,,	... 沛	,,	569
,,	... 孥	,,	940	,,	... 陪	,,	363
,,	... 努	,,	943	,,	... 培	,,	363
,,	... 弩	,,	944	,,	... 賠	,,	363
,,	... 怒	,,	947	pên	... 奔	,,	57
ou	... 歐	,,	811	,,	... 本	,,	38
,,	... 毆	,,	812				

INDEX.

p'êng	...	朋	No. 34	*Continued—*			
				pien	...	辯	No. 1099
,,	...	蓬	,, 1264	,,	...	辦	,, 1100
,,	...	逢	,, 1263	p'ien	...	偏	,, 150
,,	...	烹	,, 460	,,	...	篇	,, 151
pi	...	陛	,, 928	,,	...	騙	,, 151
,,	...	璧	,, 959	,,	...	片	,, 1164
,,	...	壁	,, 958	pin	...	賓 or 儐	,, 900
,,	...	避	,, 961	p'in	...	牝	,, 338
,,	...	必	,, 28	,,	...	貧	,, 1009
,,	...	畢	,, 173	ping	...	并	,, 796
,,	...	逼	,, 646	,,	...	兵	,, 1158
,,	...	敝	,, 925	,,	...	秉	,, 541
p'i	...	匹	,, 97	p'ing	...	憑	,, 757
,,	...	疋	,, 583	,,	...	平	,, 25
,,	...	毘	,, 166	po	...	帛	,, 303
,,	...	皮	,, 571	,,	...	撥	,, 507
,,	...	琵	,, 1241	,,	...	播	,, 610
,,	...	辟	,, 954	,,	...	波	,, 577
,,	...	劈	,, 955	,,	...	玻	,, 578
,,	...	擘	,, 956	,,	...	博	,, 401
,,	...	譬	,, 960	,,	...	搏	,, 402
piao	...	表	,, 453	,,	...	膊	,, 404
p'iao	...	票	,, 105	,,	...	薄	,, 406
pien	...	弁	,, 795	,,	...	跋	,, 573
,,	...	便	,, 398	p'o	...	叵	,, 804
,,	...	貶	,, 731	,,	...	迫	,, 645
,,	...	變	,, 1153	,,	...	坡	,, 576
,,	...	扁	,, 147	,,	...	破	,, 579
,,	...	偏	,, 151	,,	...	頗	,, 580
,,	...	編	,, 151	p'ou	...	裒	,, 761
,,	...	辨	,, 1097	,,	...	剖	,, 361
			[Continued—				

INDEX.

pu	...	捕	No. 408	sung	...	宋	No. 557
,,	...	補	,, 409	,,	...	嵩	,, 1293
,,	...	簿	,, 407	,,	...	送	,, 209
,,	...	布	,, 567	shan	...	扇	,, 1020
,,	...	部	,, 362	,,	...	陝	,, 737
p'u	...	普	,, 359	shang	...	商	,, 918
,,	...	菩	,, 360	,,	...	伺	,, 916
,,	...	鋪	,, 410	,,	...	婁	,, 132
,,	...	舖	,, 411	,,	...	賞	,, 136
,,	...	僕	,, 625	,,	...	傷	,, 1311
,,	...	撲	,, 626	,,	...	殤	,, 1313
,,	...	樸	,, 627	shao	...	勺	,, 969
sa	...	撒	,, 856	shê	...	余	,, 554
,,	...	洒	,, 101	,,	...	舍	,, 692
,,	...	薩	,, 934	,,	...	捨	,, 698
sai	...	塞	,, 527	,,	...	赦	,, 479
,,	...	賽	,, 529	,,	...	社	,, 1112
san	...	叁	,, 784	,,	...	設	,, 1221
sê	...	色	,, 1123	,,	...	折	,, 1226
,,	...	瑟	,, 1240	,,	...	射	,, 661
so	...	索	,, 451	,,	...	攝	,, 1125
,,	...	鎖	,, 1233	shên	...	深	,, 200
sou	...	叟	,, 394	,,	...	腎	,, 951
su	...	素	,, 452	,,	...	審	,, 606
,,	...	粟	,, 104	,,	...	嬸	,, 612
,,	...	訴	,, 1229	,,	...	甚	,, 1081
,,	...	蕭	628 ,, 268	shéng	...	升	,, 794
suan	...	酸	,, 1090	,,	...	陞	,, 927
sui	...	崇	,, 562	,,	...	乘	,, 537
,,	...	遂	,, 1119	,,	...	膰	,, 494
sun	...	損	,, 912	,,	...	滕	,, 496

[Continued—

INDEX.

Continued—				Continued—			
shêng	...	省	No. 1063	shou	...	受	No. 440
,,	...	剩	,, 539	,,	...	授	,, 581
shih	...	釋	,, 889	,,	...	瘦	,, 394
,,	...	商	,, 919	shu	...	束	,, 235
,,	...	適	,, 923	,,	...	黍	,, 221
,,	...	勢	,, 473	,,	...	成	,, 258
,,	...	駛	,, 1028	,,	...	庶	,, 354
,,	...	師	,, 457	,,	...	輸	,, 416
,,	...	施	,, 1102	,,	...	贖	,, 884
,,	...	是	,, 586	,,	...	恕	,, 946
,,	...	世	,, 1178	,,	...	孰	,, 467
,,	...	始	,, 694	,,	...	熟	,, 469
,,	...	矢	,, 6	,,	...	叔	,, 470
,,	...	失	,, 8	,,	...	暑	,, 1007
,,	...	士	,, 36	,,	...	署	,, 1008
,,	...	溼 or 濕	,, 47	,,	...	豎	,, 1131
,,	...	恃	,, 250	,,	...	竪	,, 1132
,,	...	侍	,, 247	,,	...	速	,, 235
,,	...	時	,, 253	,,	...	書	,, 594
,,	...	氏	,, 265	shua	...	耍	,, 107
,,	...	史	,, 391	,,	...	刷	,, 1251
,,	...	使	,, 397	shuai	...	衰	,, 760
,,	...	石	,, 563	,,	...	帥	,, 456
,,	...	市	,, 568	shuan	...	拴	,, 697
,,	...	拾	,, 696	shuang	...	爽	,, 735
,,	...	飾	,, 458	shui	...	稅	,, 1053
,,	...	尸	,, 143	shun	...	舜	,, 383
,,	...	實	,, 901	ssŭ	...	司	,, 980
shou	...	手	,, 22	,,	...	四	,, 98
,,	...	守	,, 240	,,	...	思	,, 126
,,	...	售	,, 750	,,	...	寺	,, 247
			[Continued—				[Continued—

INDEX.

Continued—				Continued—			
ssŭ	...	俟	No. 443	t'ang	...	唐	No. 330
,,	...	巳	,, 968	,,	...	帑	,, 942
,,	...	斯	,, 1083	,,	...	湯	,, 1307
,,	...	祠	,, 1111	,,	...	盪	,, 1307
,,	...	祀	,, 1113	,,	...	糖	,, 330
ta	...	答	,, 702	tao	...	島	,, 194
,,	...	踏	,, 985	,,	...	刀	,, 197
tai	...	戴	,, 346	,,	...	蹈	,, 986
,,	...	獃	,, 326	,,	...	導	,, 603
,,	...	歹	,, 686	,,	...	到	,, 425
,,	...	代	,, 675	,,	...	倒	,, 428
,,	...	貸	,, 683	,,	...	稻	,, 986
,,	...	待	,, 248	t'ao	...	套	,, 718
t'ai	...	態	,, 369	té	...	得	,, 249
,,	...	太	,, 4	t'ê	...	特	,, 252
,,	...	泰	,, 487	têng	...	登	,, 503
,,	...	臺	,, 780	,,	...	凳	,, 504
,,	...	台	,, 694	,,	...	鐙	,, 503
,,	...	抬	,, 695	,,	...	燈	,, 503
,,	...	胎	,, 694	t'êng	...	謄	,, 495
tan	...	丹	,, 787	,,	...	騰	,, 497
,,	...	单 or 單	,, 962	,,	...	籐	,, 499
,,	...	誕	,, 348	ti	...	滌	,, 447
t'an	...	探	,, 204	,,	...	滴	,, 921
,,	...	炭	,, 116	,,	...	遞	,, 1239
,,	...	貪	,, 1010	,,	...	狄	,, 664
,,	...	歎	,, 532	,,	...	弟	,, 818
tang	...	黨	,, 142	,,	...	第	,, 822
,,	...	當	,, 138	,,	...	娣	,, 824
t'ang	...	棠	,, 134	,,	...	敵	,, 926
,,	...	堂	,, 135			[Continued—	

INDEX.

				Continued—			
t'i	... 剃	No.	818	to	... 朵	No.	214
,,	... 提	,,	588	,,	... 馱	,,	1270
,,	... 梯	,,	818	t'o	... 它	,,	243
,,	... 踢	,,	1302	,,	... 駝	,,	1269
,,	... 剔	,,	1302	,,	... 馱	,,	1270
tiao	... 吊	,,	817	,,	... 託	,,	245
,,	... 刁	,,	198	,,	... 妥	,,	437
,,	... 釣	,,	976	,,	... 脫	,,	1052
t'iao	... 條	,,	447	tou	... 陡	,,	1026
tieh	... 迭	,,	211	t'ou	... 偷	,,	412
,,	... 疊	,,	642	,,	... 投	,,	1220
t'ieh	... 帖	,,	1279	tu	... 度	,,	355
,,	... 貼	,,	1280	,,	... 渡	,,	355
tien	... 典	,,	85	,,	... 瀆	,,	880
,,	... 電	,,	165	,,	... 犢	,,	881
,,	... 殿	,,	842	,,	... 牘	,,	882
,,	... 靛	,,	472	,,	... 讀	,,	885
,,	... 奠	,,	600	,,	... 突	,,	1234
,,	... 點	,,	635	,,	... 獨	,,	121
,,	... 玷	,,	1277	,,	... 篤	,,	650
t'ien	... 天	,,	10	t'u	... 土	,,	35
,,	... 添	,,	223	,,	... 荼	,,	207
,,	... 田	,,	75	,,	... 禿	,,	219
ting	... 頂	,,	1046	,,	... 兔	,,	313
,,	... 定	,,	584	,,	... 途	,,	212
t'ing	... 廷	,,	347	,,	... 徒	,,	1025
,,	... 亭	,,	462	,,	... 突	,,	1234
tiu	... 丟	,,	1000	tuan	... 叚	,,	839
to	... 奪	,,	719	,,	... 端	,,	1173
,,	... 鐸	,,	890	,,	... 短	,,	673
,,	... 墮	,,	1120	,,	... 斷	,,	654
		[Continued—					

INDEX. 115

tui	...	兒	No. 66	tsao	...	早	No. 299
t'ui	...	退	,, 279	,,	...	阜	,, 301
,,	...	腿	,, 279	,,	...	蚤	,, 240
tun	...	敦	,, 464	,,	...	蚤	,, 111
,,	...	整	,, 471	ts'ao	...	草	,, 510
t'un	...	褪	,, 279	tsé	...	仄	,, 114
tung	...	動	,, 518	,,	...	責	,, 869
,,	...	盅	,, 551	,,	...	謫	,, 922
,,	...	東	,, 720	,,	...	澤	,, 886
t'ung	...	仝	,, 689	,,	...	擇	,, 887
,,	...	同	,, 983	tsei	...	賊	,, 261
,,	...	畫	,, 1175	tsêng	...	曾	,, 1166
,,	...	筒	,, 983	tso	...	左	,, 565
tsa	...	雜	,, 535	,,	...	作	,, 1200
tsai	...	再	,, 153	tsou	...	奏	,, 485
,,	...	在	,, 743	ts'ou	...	湊	,, 485
,,	...	宰	,, 775	tsu	...	租	,, 1054
,,	...	災	,, 375	,,	...	祖	,, 1056
,,	...	哉	,, 341	,,	...	阻	,, 1058
,,	...	栽	,, 343	,,	...	族	,, 1106
,,	...	載	,, 345	,,	...	足	,, 585
ts'ai	...	才	,, 231	ts'u	...	粗	,, 1057
,,	...	材	,, 233	,,	...	醋	,, 1091
,,	...	采	,, 438	tsui	...	醉	,, 1092
,,	...	菜	,, 208	tsun	...	尊	,, 601
,,	...	猜	,, 873	,,	...	遵	,, 602
,,	...	裁	,, 342	ts'un	...	寸	,, 230
ts'an	...	殘	,, 1291	,,	...	村	,, 232
,,	...	參	,, 783	,,	...	存	,, 742
tsang	...	葬	,, 56	tsung	...	宗	,, 558

INDEX.

ts'ung	...	從	No. 1023	Continued—			
				wei	...	諉	No. 1014
,,	...	匆 or 怱	,, 1182	,,	...	味	,, 39
tzŭ	...	紫	,, 229	wên	...	溫	,, 48
,,	...	恣	,, 353	,,	...	紊	,, 936
,,	...	姿	,, 352	,,	...	問	,, 1071
,,	...	仔	,, 741	,,	...	聞	,, 1073
,,	...	笫	,, 821	,,	...	蚊	,, 937
,,	...	姊	,, 823	,,	...	刎	,, 1181
,,	...	子	,, 17	wo	...	我	,, 1031
,,	...	漬	,, 895	wu	...	午	,, 12
tz'ŭ	...	朿	,, 234	,,	...	烏	,, 191
,,	...	刺	,, 236	,,	...	舞	,, 384
,,	...	伺	,, 982	,,	...	毋	,, 1161
,,	...	辭	,, 1254	,,	...	勿	,, 1181
,,	...	賜	,, 1302	,,	...	惡	,, 1216
wan	...	挽	,, 312	ya	...	了	,, 16
,,	...	萬	,, 328	,,	...	押	,, 78
,,	...	完	,, 559	,,	...	壓	,, 382
,,	...	彎	,, 1152	,,	...	亞	,, 1215
,,	...	丸	,, 1191	yang	...	易	,, 1303
,,	...	晚	,, 312	,,	...	揚	,, 1305
wang	...	罔	,, 161	,,	...	楊	,, 1306
,,	...	往	,, 746	,,	...	央	,, 50
,,	...	妄	,, 62	,,	...	仰	,, 285
,,	...	網	,, 163	,,	...	恙	,, 1033
,,	...	王	,, 831	,,	...	洋	,, 1067
wei	...	未	,, 39	,,	...	養	,, 1037
,,	...	胃	,, 92	,,	...	陽	,, 1309
,,	...	畏	,, 167	yao	...	夭	,, 11
,,	...	委	,, 217	,,	...	杳	,, 183
,,	...	微	,, 852	,,	...	肴	,, 454
			[Continued—				[Continued—

INDEX. 117

Continued—				Continued—		
yao	... 遙	No. 844	yi	... 邑	No. 1124
,,	... 要	,, 106	,,	... 役	,, 1219
,,	... 藥	,, 1151	,,	... 胰	,, 820
,,	... 舀	,, 986	yin	... 因	,, 123
,,	... 廮	,, 106	,,	... 印	,, 287
yeh	... 冶	,, 699	,,	... 殷	,, 841
,,	... 也	,, 1177	,,	... 銀	,, 277
,,	... 葉	,, 1209	ying	... 盈	,, 351
,,	... 業	,, 624	,,	... 應	,, 754
,,	... 謁	,, 1197	,,	... 鷹	,, 755
yen	... 焉	,, 195	,,	... 鸁	,, 836
,,	... 眼	,, 269	,,	... 贏	,, 837
,,	... 延	,, 348	,,	... 塋	,, 1147
,,	... 沿	,, 364	,,	... 瑩	,, 1145
,,	... 厭	,, 381	,,	... 營	,, 1146
,,	... 雁 or 鴈	,, 753	,,	... 瑩	,, 1148
,,	... 寅	,, 1265	,,	... 熒	,, 1149
,,	... 演	,, 1267	,,	... 英	,, 50
,,	... 魇	,, 1266	,,	... 勤	,, 513
,,	... 咽	,, 123	yo	... 樂	,, 1150
,,	... 宴	,, 658	,,	... 岳	,, 1159
,,	... 晏	,, 659	,,	... 約	,, 969
,,	... 烟	,, 123	yü	... 予	,, 18
yi	... 弋	,, 255	,,	... 于	,, 21
,,	... 逸	,, 313	,,	... 宇	,, 244
,,	... 抑	,, 285	,,	... 育	,, 94
,,	... 燈	,, 779	,,	... 域	,, 315
,,	... 繹	,, 888	,,	... 蜮	,, 315
,,	... 譯	,, 891	,,	... 寓	,, 327
,,	... 驛	,, 892	,,	... 游	,, 367
,,	... 揖	,, 913	,,	... 臾	,, 395
		[Continued—			[Continued—

INDEX.

Continued—

yŭ	諭	No. 414	yu	尤	No.	68
,,	余	,, 553	,,	由	,,	76
,,	欲	,, 1003	,,	油	,,	83
,,	雨	,, 1018	,,	幽	,,	154
,,	與	,, 86	,,	郵	,,	540
,,	興	,, 88	,,	叉	,,	109
,,	餘	,, 553	,,	右	,,	564
,,	玉	,, 832	,,	友	,,	566
yüan	玄	,, 433	,,	遊	,,	843
,,	員	,, 863	,,	酉	,,	100
,,	冤	,, 313	,,	憂	,,	965
,,	緣	,, 619	,,	誘	,,	1013
,,	袁	,, 763	,,	祐	,,	1116
,,	逮	,, 770	,,	猶	,,	120
,,	怨	,, 948	,,	柚	,,	82
,,	援	,, 582	,,	優	,,	965
yŭeh	曰	,, 46	yung	永	,,	43
,,	月	,, 785	,,	勇	,,	176
,,	粵	,, 1070	,,	雍	,,	614
yŭn	允	,, 69	,,	榮	,,	1144
,,	運	,, 423	,,	塋	,,	1145
,,	勻	,, 970	,,	蠅	,,	1148
,,	孕	,, 213	,,	擁	,,	614
,,	孕	,, 420a	,,	癰	,,	1149

ERRATA.

No. 338 — for $p'in^1$ read $p'in^4$.
,, 415 — ,, $lun^{1.4}$,, $lun^{2.4}$.
,, 421 — ,, $hun^{2.3}$,, $hun^{2.4}$.

www.ingramcontent.com/pod-product-compliance
Lightning Source LLC
Chambersburg PA
CBHW022142160426
43197CB00009B/1395